THE AMERICAN UNIVERSITY
UNDERGRADUATE LAW JOURNAL

AU UNDERGRAD
LAW JOURNAL

D1458073

Masthead

Editors-In-Chief:

Harsha Mudaliar

Jack Baum

Managing Editor:

Jonathon DiPietro

Communications Coordinator:

Russell Sullivan

Column Editors:

Matthew Stefan	Business Law Column
Morgan Harris	Civil Rights Column
Ben Parsons	Constitutional Law Column
Lauren Greenberg	Criminal Law Column
Alexis Saldana	Education Law Column
Sophia Olson	Environmental Law Column
Ben Mermel	Immigration and International Law
Abbie Kitariev	Legal Theory Column

Blog Editor

Julianna Boyson

THE AMERICAN UNIVERSITY
UNDERGRADUATE LAW JOURNAL

AU UNDERGRAD
LAW JOURNAL

BUSINESS LAW

COLUMN

DO FATHERS DESERVE LONGER PATERNITY LEAVE?

BY ALICIA RIDGLEY

INTRODUCTION

Paternity leave is a highly debated topic within businesses across the country. According to researchers, paternity leave is "an approved absence from work due to the birth or adoption of a child."[1] Similar to maternity leave, fathers are granted time off from work when they adopt or their significant other gives birth to their child. It gives the family time to adjust to a new lifestyle, and spend important developmental time with their new child before creating a new type of balance between work and family. In simpler terms, this period of time where the parent gets to learn how to care for their new child and adjust their lifestyle to accommodate parenthood and being a working adult. Maternity leave is generally longer in duration and approved at greater rates than paternity leave, meaning that a paternal parent must return to work sooner than a maternal parent.

---

[1] *What is paternity leave?* HR definitions & examples, MightyRecruiter (2016),
https://www.mightyrecruiter.com/recruiter-guide/hiring-glossary-a-to-z/paternity-leave/

While paternity leave has become more popular in more recent years, there has been quite some debate over whether the paternal parent should be granted more leave or not. Some believe that legally, and in a humane stance, paternity leave should be dictated based on the family situation, and it should provide a bigger range of time off for the company and family to agree upon. Others believe that paternity leave should stay the same, and maternity leave is far more important to consider. The historical evidence and development of paternity leave have evolved over time and arguments for and against have made for a contentious discussion in today's society.

HISTORICAL EVIDENCE

For several years, particularly in this recently politically active decade, maternity leave was, and continues to be, a widely debated topic in and outside of the workplace. Naturally, in past years, society dictated that a woman's place was at home to care for the house, children, and affairs that her husband couldn't otherwise handle while he was working to provide for the family.

"'A Woman's Place is in the House' is a phrase used by misogynists to tell women that their only value is what they can do for the man who has them in their home. Women were treated as less than domestic servants, often with fewer rights than the male child they bore and were raising."[2]

---

[2] *A Woman's Place is in the House*, Green Party US (2019), https://www.gp.org/in_the_house

This is where the societal term housewife came into play. As the years went on and views on life roles began to modernize, women were integrated more into society and became an integral part of the work world. Women's workplace participation had increased significantly in 2019 from 2018, but hadn't increased much in 2019 for men.[3] As women more often received roles in higher business positions, the question of maternity leave was brought into the conversation. Oftentimes, because of unfair parental leave policies, women are forced to quit their jobs to care for newborns and children in order to make sure they get the proper care, which limits a family financially.[4] It became clear that asking women to choose between starting a family and pursuing a career was unfair and becoming increasingly unacceptable in society.

Patricia Schroder, a Democratic Congressional Representative from Colorado in 1985, worked to pass the Paternal and Disability Leave Act. She introduced the Parental and Disability Leave Act, which mandated eighteen weeks of unpaid, job-protected leave for new parents, as well as twenty-six weeks of leave to care for a sick child.[5] This provided parents with the opportunity

---

[3] *Women in the Labor Force: A Databook : BLS reports*, U.S. Bureau of Labor Statistics (2021),
https://www.bls.gov/opub/reports/womens-databook/2020/home.htm#:~:text=the%20technical%20notes.)-,Selected%20demographic%20characteristics,previous%20year%20(69.1%20percent).
[4] Kat Ventoruzzo, *Parental Leave and a Women's Attachment to the Workforce*, SOCAP Global (2020),
https://socapglobal.com/2020/01/parental-leave-and-a-womens-attachment-to-the-workforce/
[5] Megan A. Sholar, *The history of Family leave policies in the United States*, The American Historian,

to care for their child in those first few crucial weeks of life.

In 1993, the Family and Medical Leave Act was signed into law and allowed for more accessibility to maternity and paternity leave, but with guidelines such as the amount of hours worked within a company and employee count within the specific company they work for.[6] Needless to say, these bills passed for new parents provided a lot of flexibility for parents to take warranted time off to care for their new children. Although these laws were very supportive of building families, the language within the legislation does not provide guidelines for paternity leave. They support a woman's right to heal and grow, whereas men were left clueless as to their role within these laws.

Modern advocates for paternity leave have petitioned to provide more inclusive language and guidelines for working fathers across the country. The Biden Administration has led discussions with the intention of creating better standards for paternity leave that may even include compensation during the time of leave. While the conversation is beginning, it is unlikely that things will change soon. Biden's administration is working on the Build Back Better Plan, which includes important legislation supporting paternity leave, though

---

https://www.oah.org/tah/issues/2016/november/the-history-of-family-leave-policies-in-the-united-states/#:~:text=In%201985%20Representative%20Patricia%20Schroeder,the%20employee's%20own%20temporary%20disability.
[6] Family and Medical Leave Act of 1993, 29 U.S.C. §§ 2601–2654 (2006).

it could take quite some time to develop.[7] Not every decision made from a government and workplace perspective evolves and becomes perfected overnight; this is an issue that will take an extensive amount of time and effort from all parties involved to make a positive change. In other words, complex issues While this is still a work in progress amongst our government and workplaces, we continue, as a country, to advocate for supporters of federal wide paternity leave and equality surrounding paternity leave.

MODERN DAY ARGUMENTS

Given the politically active nature of our society, there has been a lot of debate as to whether or not access to paternity leave should be revised. With the modernized #MeToo movement and feminism on the rise, many individuals believe that maternity leave should take precedence. By revising the laws surrounding paternity leave, it would be diminishing a woman's right to self-care and medical leave, as some would argue in their own opinion.

"While polls show that most Americans support paid parental leave for men, cultural biases continue to obstruct its adoption despite research indicating that such policies help with everything from family finances to improving gender equity in the workplace."[8]

---

[7] Adam Bulger, *The state of Paternity Leave in America*, Fatherly (2021),
https://www.fatherly.com/love-money/paternity-leave-laws-state-us/
[8] Aimee Picchi, *America's troubled relationship with paid time off for Dads*, CBS News (2021),

Cultural and societal norms, similar to what occurred in the early 20th century, have dictated that men do not need to be present after a child's birth for as long as a woman. It would be contradictory to the gender equity standards that have been created in modern society and especially in the contemporary workplace.

An empirical analysis suggests that a majority of Americans support paternity leave as well as paid maternity and paternity leave. Despite the popularity of these programs, companies are often not fair to those who want or need to take the time off. For those companies that do offer it have seen their numbers decrease, specifically from 2010 to 2014 as rules have changed amongst workplaces. They deem it to be unfair with their policies and unsupportive of new parents trying to navigate their way through this new chapter in life.[9]

Going forward, future presidential administrations are looking to change the way companies align company-wide benefits for their employees by making sure they're legally able to take their leave and be properly compensated for it. President Biden addressed in a recent bill and State of the Union his plan to include

---

https://www.cbsnews.com/news/paternity-leave-pete-buttigieg-criticism-policy-united-states/
[9] Claire Cain Miller, *Paternity leave: The rewards and the remaining stigma*, The New York Times (2014), https://www.nytimes.com/2014/11/09/upshot/paternity-leave-the-rewards-and-the-remaining-stigma.html

better laws for family leave, including paternity leave, that will affect families positively across the country.[10]

Examining paternity leave from a different perspective, there are a select few that believe paternity leave laws should be changed. The public growth of the LGBTQ+ community has created new types of families that have impacted the societal view of a conventional family. Gay couples, transgender people, and others who wish to have children are not always afforded the benefit of having their own biological children. They tend to adopt, and in the majority of cases a couple consisting of two men will need to take time off to welcome their new baby into the family. This brings many complications with the current paternity leave laws set in place. If one paternal parent isn't offered their right to paternity leave within their company, they lose out on time with their family and the ability to adapt to a new lifestyle they will lead. More importantly, the child being brought into their family will lose out on the quality time they might need to adjust to their new home. "On average, same-sex male couples had five fewer months of paid leave than different-sex couples, while same-sex females received three fewer months than heterosexual couples, researchers said."[11] It is a power struggle between gender equality, paternal/maternal rights, and societal norms

---

[10] Lorie Konish, *Biden pushes for paid family leave in state of the Union Address*, CNBC (2022), https://www.cnbc.com/2022/03/02/biden-touts-paid-family-leave-in-state-of-the-union-address.html

[11] Kate Ryan, *Gay fathers receive less parental leave than other couples: Study*, Reuters (2019), https://www.reuters.com/article/us-global-lgbt-parentalleave/gay-fathers-receive-less-parental-leave-than-other-couples-study-idUSKCN1VQ0EX

that make the conversation more difficult and harder to come to an equal decision.

FUTURE OUTLOOK AND CONCLUSION

Looking toward the future, it is in the best interest of the American government to examine the pros and cons of paternity leave. For the majority, the best option is to make paternity leave a requirement for all businesses across the country. Utilizing the laws that are already in place, lawmakers can divulge deep into the language of each bill and make sure they understand what's important and what's in the best interest for all Americans. As long as we can agree that paternity leave has equal and important rights without diminishing the efforts done to ensure women have a prominent role in society, there can be a compromise as to how paternity and maternity leave become federalized. It would be beneficial not only to straight men, but men from different communities and all walks of life. Revising this law and supporting the efforts of fathers in and out of the workplace can teach valuable lessons and modernize our society further for future legal developments.

LIABILITY AND MANDATES: THE EFFECTS OF COVID-19 ON BUSINESSES

BY ELLA LANE

INTRODUCTION

The COVID-19 pandemic has forced us all to drastically change almost every aspect of our lives: social, work, etc., as in-person meetings became dangerous, masks became routine, and medical misinformation plagued the public.[12] Not only have individual patterns been radically altered, but businesses and other key stakeholders in our economy have also changed immensely. Businesses have been widely impacted by the COVID-19 pandemic in a number of ways: lack of staffing, COVID-19 ordinances and shutdowns, adaptations to a virtual setting, and

---

[12] KFF, COVID-19 Misinformation is Ubiquitous: 78% of the Public Believes or is Unsure About At Least One False Statement, and Nearly a Third Believe At Least Four of Eight False Statements Tested, (Nov. 8, 2021).
https://www.kff.org/coronavirus-covid-19/press-release/covid-19-misinformation-is-ubiquitous-78-of-the-public-believes-or-is-unsure-about-at-least-one-false-statement-and-nearly-at-third-believe-at-least-four-of-eight-false-statements-tested/

much more. The pandemic has created an entirely new system for businesses and practitioners of law, and one area that has had to grapple with a host of new questions is the area of liability and damages. Who, if anyone, can be held accountable for COVID-19 infections? Will accidental vs. knowing infections be treated differently? Can enforcements of vaccination and masking procedures be applied in businesses? These issues have been brought up often in court proceedings and local, state and federal legislatures over the past two years. States have taken vastly different approaches to regulating liability concerns and mandated COVID-19 requirements, like mask and vaccination mandates. States have had to take their own approaches to regulating these concerns, with little to no federal requirements from the previous administration and just a few more regulations from the current one, mostly in regards to federal workers and other federal entities.[13][14] COVID-19 litigation has also had extremely varied results from state to state, in every area from mandates to damage claims. It is pertinent to examine the differences in legislation and court proceedings from state to state and at the federal level, and by reviewing pending cases and past precedent we can theorize how businesses will be impacted by the several legal challenges posed by the COVID-19 pandemic.

---

[13] Department of Health and Human Services, Report to Congress: COVID-19 Strategic Testing Plan, (May 24, 2020). https://www.democrats.senate.gov/imo/media/doc/COVID%2 0National%20Diagnostics%20Strategy%2005%2024%202020 %20v%20FINAL.pdf
[14] 86 C.F.R. § 50989.1 (2021).

WHO CAN BE HELD LIABLE:
EMPLOYERS, EMPLOYEES, CONSUMERS

State legislatures across the country have been quick to enact liability immunity policies, statutes that shield certain individuals or groups from lawsuits, for whoever they deem to be a protected individual or group. Some states and districts have created their own liability protection policies, but have focused mostly on protecting first responders and care providers. For example, the District of Columbia provided liability protections for these groups from March 2020 until the COVID-19 Response Supplemental Emergency Amendment Act of 2020 expired in April 2021.[15] Governors and legislatures, especially those in deep-red bastions like Alabama and Indiana, have also created immunity policies. These tend to focus more on protecting businesses from injury or death claims to incentivize reopenings. Alabama's SB 30 provided liability protections for any business, church, educational or government entity, healthcare provider, and cultural institution from claims for injury as a result of COVID-19 until it expired in December of 2021.[16] Indiana's Senate Bill 1, which gave businesses civil tort immunity except in the case of gross negligence or willful wanton misconduct, bans class action lawsuits for COVID-19 related injury claims.[17] Both bills provide protection from injury claims as a result of provision of personal protective equipment, and provide effective immunity from consumer based claims of injury and others.

---

[15]DC Act. § 67.4178.401 (2020).

[16] SB. 30, Reg. Sess. 2020. (Al. 2020). (enacted).

[17] SB. 1, 122nd Cong. 1st Sess. (In. 2021).

Despite this, there are still routes employees can take to file a claim. Neither Alabama nor Indiana restricted employment claims in their acts— opening an avenue for workers to file COVID-19 related claims in these states. Other states, such as California, have been especially open to COVID-19 related litigation. In See's Candies Inc. v. Superior Court, a California Court of Appeals ruled in favor of a See's Candies employee who sued her employer under the pretext that she contracted COVID-19 and spread it to her husband, who later died of the virus, due to improper safety measures on the part of the company.[18] She filed a wrongful death lawsuit, but the defendants argued for a dismissal based on provisions included in the California Workers Compensation Act.[19] The provision, called "exclusive remedy," allows for quick compensation for workers regardless of negligence on the part of the employer. In exchange, the employer is shielded from liability outside of the compensation paid to the employee. The court decided that the exclusive remedy doctrine is a contract only between the employer and employee— meaning that the husband of the plaintiff's injuries cannot be covered by exclusive remedy. This ruling opens the door for injury claims from both employees and non-employees towards businesses in California, especially in claims of negligence or wrongful death. This trend could be followed in other states with exclusive remedy doctrines, like North Carolina and Connecticut, which are fairly common in many state's workers compensation codes.

---

[18] See's Candies Inc. v. Superior Court Cal. App. 1076 (Cal. 2021).

[19] Cal. Code. Reg. California Workers' Compensation Act 3 § 3600.

States vary widely on legal issues regarding negligence codifications. Tennessee decided in Lazenby v. Universal Underwriters Insurance Co. to allow indemnification for assessment of punitive damages.[20] This means that an insurer is liable to pay punitive damages on behalf of the insured in the state of Tennessee.[21] However, in Florida, courts reached an opposite decision that did not recognize the coverage of punitive damages in Northwestern National Casualty Co. v. McNulty.[22] This discrepancy could result in COVID-19 negligence claims and insurance coverage between the states, of which we are already seeing. Under the *Lazenby* interpretation, insurance companies may be liable to pay punitive damages for outrageously negligent cases with blatant disregard for public health, perhaps in incidents like purposeful coughing in the faces of the elderly, a charge that has come up often in recent months.[23] Under the *McNulty* interpretation, said companies may not have to cover wanton or reckless negligence. Discrepancy between states and current lack of precedent on COVID-19 negligence cases leaves space for states to take up either interpretation in ruling on pandemic negligence cases.

---

[20] Lazenby v. Universal Underwriters Co. Tenn. Sup. Ct. 383 S.W.2d 1 (Tenn. 1964)

[21] Barry Kutun, Insurance Against the Assessment of Punitive Damages, 20 U. Miami L. Rev. 192 (1965). https://repository.law.miami.edu/umlr/vol20/iss1/9

[22] Northwestern National Casualty Co. v. McNulty 307 F.2d 432 (US 5th Cir. 1962).

[23] Pennsylvania man faces charges for deliberately coughing near elderly man who was wearing a medical face mask CBS 42, (Mar. 24, 2020). https://www.cbs42.com/news/pennsylvania-man-faces-charges -for-deliberately-coughing-near-elderly-man-who-was-wearin g-medical-face-mask/

Finally, COVID-19 coverage by insurance companies is itself questioned. In Kenyon v. Security Ins. Co. of Hartford, an insurance company, had to pay damages because of the broad coverage plan it gave to the defendant, and the court noted that a more specific plan could have helped the company avoid paying damages.[24] Some insurance companies are already reevaluating coverage for COVID-19 related illness in their plans. Shifts in coverage of COVID-19 related illness may change the out-of-pocket expenses for individuals and businesses.

COVID-19 EXPOSURE

Most COVID-19 related lawsuits charging a business or individual are filed as negligence, wrongful death, and negligent personal injury claims. These sorts of claims typically imply accidental or reckless and wanton behavior, and they are almost always brought to civil courts. There have been more questions about whether a person can be tried criminally if they intentionally infected a person. Many Americans already have been criminally prosecuted for coronavirus related crimes, and many have called for the prosecution of former President Trump for rampant COVID-19 breakouts at rallies and White House events. Former Attorney General Jeffery Rosen encouraged enforcement officials in a memorandum to prosecute those who intentionally try to spread the disease.[25] As stated in the memorandum,

---

[24] Kenyon v. Security Ins. Co. of Hartford 626 N.Y.S.2d 347 (Ny. 1993).
[25] Memorandum from the Deputy Attorney General to All Heads of Law Enforcement Components, Heads of Litigating Divisions. and United States Attorneys (Mar. 24, 2020). https://www.justice.gov/file/1262771/download

COVID-19 qualifies as a "biological agent" and therefore could implicate someone for a terrorism charge.[26] The most common charge under this area would be threats of terrorism, which is a criminal offense in many states. In addition to terrorism, individuals have wracked up charges like assault and battery, reckless endangerment, harassment, disorderly conduct, and a variety of violations of state communicable disease laws.[27] These criminal charges have affected businesses as well, especially during the most intense months of the pandemic. Many states have criminally charged business owners for noncompliance with COVID-19 laws, and individuals and employees can be charged for disorderly conduct for noncompliance with state regulations. This era of the pandemic seems to be coming to an end, but the precedent set for criminally charging business owners and other individuals will persist for future public health crises.

VACCINE, MASKING, TESTING REQUIREMENTS

Vaccine requirements have existed in American culture since George Washington had his continental army inoculated against smallpox in 1777. Today, vaccine requirements have drawn heavy criticism from politicians, business leaders, and average citizens. Conversely, many major companies like Blackstone, AT&T, and Ford Motors have initiated some sort of

---

[26] Crimes and Criminal Procedure: Biological Weapons 18 U.S.C. §178 (1) (2010).

[27] Robert Anello, "Achoo . . . So Sue Me!": Criminal Liability For Spreading A Virus (Dec. 16, 2020).
https://www.forbes.com/sites/insider/2020/12/16/achoo----so-sue-me-criminal-liability-for-spreading-a-virus/?sh=8db07a628974

vaccine mandate, as did President Biden when he signed an executive order to require federal employees to be vaccinated. Vaccine mandates have been considered constitutional by several state judiciary bodies for a very long time— the basis of most current COVID-19 suits dates from 1905. In *Jacobson v. Massachusetts*, the Supreme Court upheld the right for a small town to institute a smallpox vaccine mandate for all adult citizens.[28] Further, a *Prince v. Massachusetts* opinion held that "A parent cannot claim freedom from compulsory vaccination for the child more than for himself on religious grounds. The right to practice religion freely does not include liberty to expose the community or the child to communicable disease or the latter to ill health or death," implying that even religious exemptions do not always have to be accepted.[29] This opinion was also reflected in *Harris v. University of Massachusetts, Lowell,* where a US District Court decided that state universities are under no obligation to allow for religious exemptions to vaccines.[30] The UC has extended this rationale on the behalf of private entities, notably in *Beckerich v. St. Elizabeth Medical Center*, where a District Court judge wrote "if an employee believes his or her individual liberties are more important than legally permissible conditions on his or her employment, that employee can and should choose to exercise another individual liberty, no less significant—the right to seek other employment."[31] There is clear precedent that vaccine mandates are

[28] Jacobson v. Massachusetts, 197 U.S. 11 (1905)
[29] Prince v. Massachusetts, 321 U.S. 158 (1944)
[30] Harris v. University of Massachusetts, Lowell 2021 WL 3848012 (D. Ma. 2021)
[31] Beckerich v. St. Elizabeth Medical Center 2021 WL 4398027, (E.D Ky. 2021)

constitutional— therefore public and private entities are well within their right to require them.

Most of the cases above rely on the necessity to protect a community from communicable disease. The *Jacobson* decision promotes the idea that a community has a number of rights to initiate policies that protect their members from communicable disease, especially in cases of increased contagion and mortality— which means a broad interpreter of *Jacobson* could reasonably extend this decision to protect masking and testing mandates. Most courts have used *Jacobson* to declare such mandates constitutional— drawing the ire of so-called First amendment enthusiasts. However, the argument that such mandates violate the First are unfounded as masking mandates cover the entirety of the population, meaning that there is no basis of violation as no one group was singled out based on membership of a protected class. Private organizations are unheld to the constraints of the constitution, and are fully within their right to implement masking mandates themselves, even without local or state ordinances.

CONCLUSION

The pandemic presents many new challenges that corporations and legal jurisdictions must face in the coming years. Looking back to established precedent can help businesses and legal practitioners navigate this difficult time, and increased litigation in this era will create new precedents that will permanently shift the way society deals with communicable disease claims and mandates in the future.

NEXUS AND THE SUPREME COURT

BY MATTHEW STEFAN

INTRODUCTION AND CONTEXTUALIZATION

The Constitution establishes that Congress has the power to "to lay and collect taxes, duties, imposts, and excises [...]."[32] Taxation has been subject to constitutional scrutiny throughout the history of the United States. In the recent landmark decision *Wayfair v. South Dakota* by the United States Supreme Court, the Court overturned their previous holding in both *Quill Corp. v. North Dakota* and *National Bellas Hess, Inc. v. Department of Revenue of Illinois* establishing that the "physical-presence rule" for taxation is inappropriate.

THE "DORMANT" COMMERCE CLAUSE DOCTRINE

The Commerce Clause provides the Congress the responsibility to "regulate commerce [...] among the

---

[32] U.S. CONST. art. I, § 8, cl. 1.

several states."[33] In the Court's majority opinion in *Gibbons v. Ogden,* Justice Marshall states explicitly that commerce "must be placed in the hands of agents or lie dormant."[34] "Dormant" or "negative" interpretations of the Commerce Clause have been frequent topics of debate among legal scholars, but generally the doctrine is summarized in that the Commerce Clause "[prohibits …] states passing legislation that discriminates against or excessively burdens interstate commerce."[35] This doctrine has had fierce opponents on the bench including Justice Antonin Scalia who believed the "dormant" Commerce Clause to be "judicial fraud" and "utterly illogical."[36] The dormant Commerce Clause is cited and recited across the board in many landmark taxation cases.

NEXUS AND THE COURT BROADLY

Taxation is an extremely complex issue in the eyes of the Court and is controlled majoritively by "nexus". Sales tax nexus describes the relationship between a given jurisdiction and a tax payee.[37] The Court determined in 1872 that the "extent of taxation is unlimited, where the subjects to which it applies are within her jurisdiction."[38] Further, in New York, L.E. & W.R. Co. v. Pennsylvania, the court solidifies this principle and asserts that "no

---

[33] U.S. CONST. art. I, § 8, cl. 3.

[34] Gibbons v. Ogden, 22 U.S. 1, 189 (1824).

[35] *Commerce Clause*, CORNELL LAW SCHOOL. (2021), https://www.law.cornell.edu/wex/commerce_clause

[36] Comptroller of the Treasury of Md. v. Wynne, 575 U.S. ___ (2015).

[37] *What is Nexus?* SALES TAX INSTITUTE. (2021), https://www.salestaxinstitute.com/sales_tax_faqs/what_is_nexus

[38] Erie R. Co. v. Pennsylvania, 82 U.S. 300 (1872).

principle is better settled than the power of a state, even its power of taxation, in respect to property, is limited to such as within its jurisdiction."[39] The court reaffirmed this idea in another landmark tax case, *Miller Brothers Co. v. Maryland*, stating that "due process requires some definite link, some minimum connection, between a state and the person, property or transaction it seeks to tax."[40] The ideas of "definite link" and "minimum connection" permeate significantly through nexus related jurisprudence culminating most recently in the landmark *Wayfair* case in 2018.

The Court also held in *Complete Auto Transit v. Brady*, that taxes are acceptable "when the tax is applied to an activity with a substantial nexus with the taxing State, is fairly apportioned, does not discriminate against interstate commerce, and is fairly related to the services provided by the state."[41] The notion of "substantial nexus" is also utilized repeatedly in the court's decision to overturn their precedent set in the most recent *Quill* decision.

NEXUS AND THE COURT TODAY

In 1967 and the years prior, National Bellas Hess, a mail-order catalogue company, was headquartered in Missouri. Doing business as a mail-order corporation, customers from other states could find products in catalogue and order them for delivery to their home. Prior to a decision by the Supreme Court of Illinois, National Bellas Hess did not have to collect and remit

[39] New York, L.E. & W. R. Co. v. Pennsylvania, 153 U.S. 628, 646 (1894).
[40] Miller Brothers Co. v. Maryland, 347 U.S. 340, 345 (1954).
[41] Complete Auto Transit, Inc. v. Brady, 430 U.S. 274 (1977).

Illinois state sales tax when they sold goods to residents of the state. Upon hearing the case in 1967, the Supreme Court of the United States found that "the Commerce Clause prohibits a State from imposing the duty of use tax collection and payment upon a seller whose only connection with customers in the State is by common carrier or by mail."[42] This decision remains in line with the courts prior determinations. Notably though, the dissenting opinions in *Bellas Hess* provide interesting insight into the changing attitudes of the Court. Justice Fortas offers the notion that "there should be no doubt that this large-scale, systematic, continuous solicitation of the Illinois consumer market is sufficient "nexus" to require Bellas Hess to collect from Illinois customers and to remit the use tax…"[43] This attitude represents a shift towards a system in which simply conducting business within a state, even without the presence of a physical operation, is enough to establish a nexus, particularly where there are systematic efforts to target the consumers within the state.

Later, in 1992, the court again approached this issue. The facts in Quill Corp. v. North Dakota are very similar to those in *Bellas Hess*. Indeed, the mail order company was compelled by the state to collect and remit sales tax. In the North Dakota Supreme Court, the majority rejected the precedent set in *Bellas Hess*, citing "tremendous social, economic, commercial, and legal innovation."[44] Indeed, this innovation was concurrent

---

[42] National Bellas Hess v. Department of Revenue, 386 U.S. 756 (1967).
[43] 386 U.S. at 762.
[44] State ex rel. Heitkamp v. Quill Corp., 470 N.W.2d 203 (1991).

with the time that had elapsed in the 24 years between *Bellas Hess* and the North Dakota decision in *Quill*.

Empirically, the population of America during that time period grew by more than 50 million, nearly every economic indicator positively increased in a substantial way, and the entire world underwent a period of massive innovation.[45] More subjectively, these changes resulted in a shift in the very cultural fabric of America. The late 1960's and 70's provided a "transformation of values" towards a society that represents "expressive individualism."[46]

In 1992, the Supreme Court overruled the North Dakota decision holding that "the Due Process Clause does not bar enforcement of the State's use tax against Quill" and "the State's enforcement of the use tax against Quill places an unconstitutional burden on interstate commerce."[47] Despite the fact that the Court overrules the initial decision they do acknowledge the reasoning for the prior decision. In the majority opinion, authored by Justice Stevens, the Court "agree[s] with much of the state court's reasoning."[48] This statement is fundamental to inferring that the Majority understands the need for progress in the law as it relates to correlates to changes in society. Despite not overturning *Bellas Hess*, the court does acknowledge in their holding that the "Court's due process jurisprudence has evolved substantially since

---

[45] *In a Lifetime,* FORBES MAG. (Oct 1, 2021), https://www.forbes.com/johnhancock/in-a-lifetime-work/#56e8492ae65c.

[46] David Yankelovich, *How American Individualism is Evolving,* THE PUBLIC PERSPECTIVE. Feb.-Mar. 1998 at 1, 5.

[47] Quill Corp. v. North Dakota, 504 U.S. 298 (1992).

[48] *Quill,* 504 U.S. at 302.

Bellas Hess, abandoning formalistic tests focused on a defendant's presence within a State in favor of a more flexible inquiry into whether a defendant's contacts with the forum made it reasonable, in the context of the federal system of Government, to require it to defend the suit in that State."[49] The Court's subtle movement with the times is obvious in their majority opinion, even though the outcome of this case does not represent a complete shift.

In *Quill,* the Court also establishes a fundamental difference between the due process and Commerce Clause requirements for nexus. While the state court suggested the clauses to be identical, the Supreme Court rejected this proposition offering that "due process centrally concerns the fundamental fairness of governmental activity [, while,] the Commerce Clause and its nexus requirement are informed not so much by concerns about fairness for the individual defendant as by structural concerns about the effects of state regulation on the national economy."[50] This reading allows the Court a broader understanding and more easily applicable standard than that of the precedent set in *Bellas Hess* and prior cases.

The Court also directly mentions the role of the negative Commerce Clause doctrine in establishing nexus. In the opinion of the Court, Justice Stevens writes that "under the Articles of Confederation, state taxes and duties hindered and suppressed interstate commerce; the Framers intended the Commerce Clause as a cure for these structural ills. It is in this light that we have interpreted the negative implication of the Commerce

---

[49] *Quill,* 504 U.S. at 298.
[50] *Quill,* 504 U.S. at 312.

Clause. Accordingly, we have ruled that that Clause prohibits discrimination against interstate commerce and bars state regulations that unduly burden interstate commerce."[51] The explicit mention of the negative Commerce Clause serves as an important insight and notion in the Court's subsequent decisions regarding nexus and state tax laws. Indeed, the application of the negative commerce doctrine serves as the establishment of this idea as the foundation of subsequent litigation related to nexus on interstate taxation.

26 years following *Quill* and 51 years after *Bellas Hess*, the court approached this issue again. The significant and fundamental changes between 1992 and 2018 were equally significant to those between the decisions in *Bellas Hess* and *Quill*. As the rise of e-commerce captured much of the American market, many of these e-commerce giants were not collecting taxes in states where they conducted business. In South Dakota alone, the Court "estimates revenue loss at $48 to $58 million annually,"[52] as a result of the decisions in *Quill* and *Bellas Hess*. Considering these facts, the South Dakota legislature imposed an Act that requires out-of-state sellers under certain parameters to collect and remit state sales tax.[53] Wayfair Inc., an e-commerce corporation with no physical real-property presence in South Dakota, falls into the group outlined within the statute.

After hearing oral arguments in *Wayfair*, the Supreme Court held that "Each year, the physical presence rule becomes further removed from economic reality and

---

[51] *Quill*, 504 U.S. at 312.

[52] South Dakota v. Wayfair, Inc., 585 U.S. ___ (2018).

[53] S. D. Codified Laws §§10–45–2, 10–45–4 (2010 and Supp. 2017).

results in significant revenue losses to the States. These critiques underscore that the physical presence rule, both as first formulated and as applied today, is an incorrect interpretation of the Commerce Clause."[54] The Court clearly identifies that the need for physical presence simply is not cohesive with the economic realities of the 21st century. The Court further determines that "*Quill* is flawed on its own terms [... and] creates rather than resolves market distortions."[55] Both components of this statement represent a fundamental change in understanding between the decisions in *Quill* and *Wayfair*. Because the *Quill* decision meant that corporations with no physical presence in the state did not have to collect sales tax, it actually benefited consumers to shop with these types of businesses. The Court goes on to explain that "modern e-commerce does not align analytically with a test that relies on the sort of physical presence defined in *Quill*. In a footnote, *Quill* rejected the argument that 'title to 'a few floppy diskettes' present in a State' was sufficient to constitute a 'substantial nexus.' But it is not clear why a single employee or a single warehouse should create a substantial nexus while 'physical' aspects of pervasive modern technology should not."[56] Clearly here, the Court acknowledges nexus through internet presence.

In concurrence, Justice Thomas commented that "a quarter century of experience has convinced me that *Bellas Hess* and *Quill* 'can no longer be rationally justified.' The same is true for this Court's entire negative Commerce Clause jurisprudence."[57] It is

---

[54] *Wayfair*, 585 U.S. at ___.
[55] *Wayfair*, 585 U.S. at ___.
[56] *Wayfair*, 585 U.S. at ___.
[57] *Wayfair*, 585 U.S. at ___.

interesting to note Justice Thomas's rejection of the precedent and of the negative Commerce Clause. Further, Justice Gorsuch comments that "for years [the courts] have enforced a judicially created tax break for out-of-state Internet and mail-order firms at the expense of in-state brick-and-mortar rivals."[58] This importantly identifies the flaws in the *Quill* decision that establish a *de facto* tax break and advantage for e-commerce corporations.

Dissenting, Justices Roberts, Kagan, and Sotomayor make several interesting notes about their reasoning for not overturning the decision in *Quill*. Justice Roberts comments that "the Court breezily disregards the costs that its decision will impose on retailers. Correctly calculating and remitting sales taxes on all e-commerce sales will likely prove baffling for many retailers."[59] Justice Roberts goes on to mention how the burden of the Court's decision will fall disproportionately on small businesses. It is interesting to see such a perspective from the bench that indicates a protectionist stance on small businesses and retailers in America.

JURISPRUDENCE FOR A CHANGING AMERICA

In a 1789 letter to James Madison, Thomas Jefferson writes that "no society can make a perpetual constitution, or even a perpetual law. The earth belongs always to the living generation."[60] Jefferson acknowledges that there is a significant need for the law to modernize in tandem with the deep and fundamental changes in cultural

---

[58] *Wayfair*, 585 U.S. at ___.
[59] *Wayfair*, 585 U.S. at ___.
[60] Letter from Thomas Jefferson to James Madison (Sept. 7, 1789) (on file with the Princeton University Press).

principles as a result of innovation. The Court, in the *Wayfair* decision, explicitly cites the need for the law to adapt to the changing realities of the Internet and e-commerce in our society. Citing Justice Jackson from a 1950 decision, Justice Thomas states in his *Wayfair* concurring opinion that "it is never too late to "surrende[r] former views to a better considered position."[61] Indeed, the Court must continually be willing, as they were in *Wayfair,* to consider alternative views that more appropriately mesh with the realities of the present day.

---

[61] *Wayfair*, 585 U.S. at ___.

THE AMERICAN UNIVERSITY
UNDERGRADUATE LAW JOURNAL

AU UNDERGRAD
LAW JOURNAL

CIVIL RIGHTS

LAW

COLUMN

DOBBS v. JACKSON WOMEN'S HEALTH: ABORTION RIGHTS THREATENED BY THE POSSIBLE OVERTURNING OF ROE

BY EMMA MILOGLAV

INTRODUCTION

Dobbs v. Jackson Women's Health Organization, argued in front of the Supreme Court on December 1, 2022, has the potential to overturn 50 years of precedent set by *Roe v. Wade*.[62,63] Jackson Women's Health Organization, a clinic and abortion facility in Jackson, Mississippi, challenged the constitutionality of Mississippi's Gestational Age Act in March 2018. The Act prohibited abortions after 15 weeks with the exception of medical

---

[62] Dobbs v Jackson Women's Health Organization 19-1392 (2021)
[63] Roe v Wade 410 U.S. 113 (1973)

emergencies or fetal abnormalities. The case was appealed to the Supreme Court in June 2020.[64]

On July 22, 2021, the petitioner, Thomas Dobbs, filed a brief asking the Court to consider whether or not to overturn *Roe v. Wade*[65] and *Planned Parenthood v. Casey*.[66] The Supreme Court elected to answer the question: Are all pre-viability prohibitions on elective abortions unconstitutional?[67]

If the Supreme Court holds that pre-viability prohibitions on abortion are constitutional, states will have the option to create further bans of abortion that will put the lives and rights of women throughout the country at risk.

DEFINITIONS

In order to understand the abortion case this article discusses, it is important to first understand the definitions of the following words and concepts surrounding abortion law.
First, the parties often address the idea of *viability* and *previability*. Viability is the fetus' ability to survive independently from the mother's womb.[68] This typically

---

[64] Andrew Hamm, Dobbs v. Jackson Women's Health Organization SCOTUSblog, https://www.scotusblog.com/case-files/cases/dobbs-v-jackson-womens-health-organization/ (last visited Feb 27, 2022).
[65] Id.
[66] Supreme Court of the United States, https://www.supremecourt.gov/DocketPDF/19/19-1392/184703/20210722161332385_19-1392BriefForPetitioners.pdf (last visited Feb 27, 2022).
[67] Dobbs v. Jackson Women's Health, *supra*, note 1
[68] Elizabeth Chloe Romanis, Is 'viability' viable? abortion, conceptual confusion and the law in England and Wales and

occurs at the 24 week mark of a pregnancy. Hence, pre-viability is the period before that mark when the fetus cannot survive without the mother.[69]

Second, the *undue burden test*, established in *Planned Parenthood v. Casey*,[70] states that "an undue burden arises if the purpose or effect of the state restriction on abortion has placed a substantial obstacle on someone seeking an abortion of a non-viable fetus."[71] Some obstacles that can qualify as an undue burden include parental consent for minors, spousal notification, waiting periods, and distances to clinics.

Third, an important legal definition to know is *stare decisis*. Stare decisis, translated into "to stand by things decided," is the principle of using precedent in order to decide new cases.[72] The Court will look at previous, similar cases and adhere to that case's rationale when coming to a new decision. In order for the Court to overlook precedent and make a decision that overruled the prior case, there must be new circumstances that demonstrate the previous ruling was "unworkable or are badly reasoned."[73]

---

the United States OUP Academic (2020), https://academic.oup.com/jlb/article/7/1/lsaa059/5918485 (last visited Feb 27, 2022).

[69] Id.

[70] Planned Parenthood of Southeastern Pennsylvania, 505 U.S. 833 (1992)

[71] Undue burden, Legal Information Institute, https://www.law.cornell.edu/wex/undue_burden (last visited Feb 27, 2022).

[72] Stare decisis, Legal Information Institute, https://www.law.cornell.edu/wex/stare_decisis (last visited Feb 27, 2022).

[73] Id.

Finally, because both *Roe v. Wade* and *Planned Parenthood v. Casey* rests on the 14th Amendment, understanding its language is crucial. The pertinent part of the amendment states "Nor shall any state deprive any person of life, liberty, or property, without due process of law; nor deny to any person within its jurisdiction the equal protection of the laws."[74]

BACKGROUND

The petitioners in this case strongly advocate for the overturning of two of the most influential abortion cases the Supreme Court has ever seen: *Roe v. Wade*, decided in 1973, and *Planned Parenthood of Southeastern Pennsylvania v. Casey*, decided in 1992.

Roe v. Wade was introduced after a Texas law made abortions illegal. In 1970, Jane Roe, a pregnant women seeking an abortion, filed a lawsuit against Henry Wade, the district attorney of Dallas County, claiming that the state laws were unconstitutional as they abridged her right to privacy.[75] The case was appealed until the Supreme Court decided to examine whether the Constitution recognizes a woman's right to terminate her pregnancy by abortion. The Court ruled that the right to privacy that protects a pregnant woman's choice to have an abortion is inherent in the due process clause of the 14th Amendment and this Texas law violated that right. The justices also created a legal framework for when the state can regulate abortion based on the trimester system of pregnancy.[76] *Roe v. Wade* has set the precedent for

---

[74] U.S. Const. amend. XIV, § 2.
[75] Roe v. Wade 410 U.S. 113 (1973)
[76] Id.

abortion rights for 50 years and is considered one of the very few watershed cases in the Court's history. Every other abortion case that has come to the Court is considered in the context of *Roe v. Wade.*

The second major abortion case, *Planned Parenthood of Southeastern Pennsylvania v. Casey*, was introduced to the Supreme Court in 1992. This case was introduced after the passage of a 1988 Pennsylvania law that required information consent, parental or spousal notification, and a 24 hour waiting period prior to any abortion procedure.[77] Several abortion clinics challenged these provisions and the Supreme Court considered whether the Pennsylvania law violated the precedent set by *Roe v. Wade.* The Court reaffirmed *Roe* and established the undue burden standard for any abortion restrictions. The Court also changed their framework from trimesters, established in *Roe*, to viability.[78] This case set the precedent for the undue burden test and viability, both of which have been used to evaluate abortion restrictions to this day.

The Court has ruled in the favor of familial privacy for decades in cases such as *Griswold v Connecticut* in 1965 which guaranteed the right of married couples to use contraceptives.[79] *Loving v. Virginia* in 1967 allowed for the marriage of interracial couples.[80] *Wisconsin v. Yoder* in 1972 granted families the ability to decide if their children attended school due to religious reasons.[81]

---

[77] Planned Parenthood of Southeastern Pennsylvania, 505 U.S. 833 (1992)
[78] Id.
[79] Griswold v. Connecticut, 381 U.S. 479 (1965)
[80] Loving v. Virginia, 388 U.S. 1, 87 S. Ct. 1817 (1967)
[81] Wisconsin v. Yoder, 406 U.S. 205 (1972)

Ultimately, all these cases demonstrate how the right to privacy in familial and personal matters has been guaranteed time and time again by the Court.

ORAL ARGUMENTS

Dobbs v. Jackson Women's Health Organization was argued on December 1st, 2021. Arguments were made by Scott G. Stewart, on behalf of the petitioner, Julie Rikelman, on behalf of the respondent, and solicitor general for the Department of Justice Elizabeth B. Prelogar, as an amicus curiae for the respondent.[82]

All three attorneys addressed four main topics in their arguments: the constitution's stance on abortion, stare decisis and the overturning of precedent, viability as a workable legal framework, and the philosophical versus practical context of abortion.

First, the right to abortion is not explicitly guaranteed in the Constitution. Stewart argues that because the Constitution is "scrupulously neutral" on the issue of abortion, there is no basis to support the decisions in *Roe* and *Casey*. Ultimately, Stewart argues that because the Constitution does not give a clear answer, the Court should remain neutral, leaving the decision of abortion rights to the states.[83]

Rikelman and Preloger disagree, stating that the Constitution is not neutral on the right to abortion, privacy, autonomy, and liberty. Chief Justice Roberts asked the two attorneys to point to the Constitutional

---

[82] Dobbs v Jackson Women's Health Organization 19-1392 (2021)
[83] Id.

right that protects the right to abortion. The attorneys
responded that abortion is guaranteed by the right to
liberty guaranteed in the 14th amendment. Liberty
includes the right to physical autonomy and family
decisions and that is how the Court has interpreted the
14th amendment for 100 years, applying a higher level
of generality to cases involving family, marriage, and
child bearing.

Second, the petitioners strongly advocate for overturning
Roe and *Casey*. The arguments around stare decisis in
Dobbs v. Jackson presents the question: why should the
Court ignore the precedents of *Roe* and Casey in
deciding *Dobbs*? Stewart makes the argument that the
decisions in *Roe* and *Casey* were egregiously wrong,
comparing them to *Plessy v. Ferguson*[84] and *Dred Scott
v. Sandford*.[85] He says that the Court was mistaken in
their decisions, claiming Casey failed because of new
science and medicine.[86] Justice Sotomayor pushes back
on the idea of the Court overturning precedent simply
because of political push back.[87] She states, "how will
the Court survive" if the people believe the Court makes
their decisions based on new laws or political tension.[88]

Rikelman rejects this idea, stating that stare decisis
presents a high bar.[89] The Court has never overruled
precedent just because some people viewed a previous
precedent as wrong. The Court requires special

---

[84] Plessy v Ferguson, 163 U.S. 537 (1896)
[85] Dred Scott v Sandford, 60 U.S. 393 (1856)
[86] Dobbs v Jackson Women's Health Organization 19-1392
(2021)
[87] Id.
[88] Id.
[89] Id.

justification and new information in order to go against precedent and the state has shown neither in their arguments. Nothing about this case is different than *Casey* and therefore stare decisis stands.[90]

In order to understand the extent of stare decisis, Justice Breyer asked Ms. Preloger if the Court can ever overrule a case just because it is egregiously wrong, citing *Plessy v. Ferguson* as an example.[91] Preloger stands strong on the argument that the Court has never overruled just because something was wrong, as they always consider new facts or context and always apply stare decisis. This is what the Court did in *Casey* and is what Preloger argues they should do today for *Dobbs*.[92]

Third, the Court considered viability as the legal line for abortion restrictions. Mr. Stewart argues that that viability line is arbitrary, neither rooted in science or tethered to the Constitution, and therefore it is not a line that can be drawn. He argues that this is a legislative line so it would be improper for the Court to rule on specifically pre-viability abortion bans.[93]

During Mrs. Rikelman's arguments, the justices asked if there was really a difference between banning abortion at 24 weeks verses 14 weeks. Rikelman focused on the reliance on the 24 week line. She stated that people who need abortions after the first 15 weeks are in the most challenging circumstances; if they are denied this

[90] Dobbs v Jackson Women's Health Organization 19-1392 (2021)
[91] Plessy v Ferguson, 163 U.S. 537 (1896)
[92] Dobbs v Jackson Women's Health Organization 19-1392 (2021)
[93] Id.

decision they will suffer severe consequences.[94] The data presented in the respondent's brief shows how abortion is critical in a women's equal participation in society and therefore the establishment of the 24 week viability line is crucial. She also stressed that without drawing a viability line there is no stopping point when states can ban abortion; at 15, 12, or even 6 weeks. When explicitly asked to defend the viability argument, Mrs. Preloger states there is "no line more principled or workable than viability."[95] Viability is grounded in science, as 24 weeks is when the fetus can survive on its own and does not delve into the philosophical questions about when life begins.

Finally, the attorneys presented their arguments about how abortion is viewed in society, its practical effects, the reliance women have on this right, and even some philosophical arguments made on behalf of Mr. Stewart. Stewart began his oral arguments by stating that there was no right to end human life, that the abortion procedure is brutal, and that "matters of conciousness" that implicate human life must be determined by the people, not the courts.[96] He explained in questioning how advancements in medicine and knowledge about fetal pain and personhood show how egregiously wrong *Casey* was.[97] Justice Sotomayor pushed back on these claims stating how only a small fringe of doctors believe that fetal pain is founded in science.[98] Justice Bryer also pushed back on the religious aspects of this argument,

---

[94] Id.

[95] Id.

[96] Id.

[97] Dobbs v Jackson Women's Health Organization 19-1392 (2021)

[98] Id.

asking if any secular philosophers believe life begins at conception.[99] Stewart responded "maybe."[100]

While Stewart focused on the philosophical, Rikelman and Preloger focused on the real life reliance women have on their right to abortion, the burdens of pregnancy and parenting, as well as the dangers of child bearing and birth. Preloger argued the greatest reliance is the individual reliance of women and their partners on their control over whether or not to have a child. This gives women reproductive control and control over their own lifestyles. One in four women have had an abortion and women continue to rely on this right to control their lives and their bodies.[101]

CONCLUSION

The decision for *Dobbs v. Jackson* is expected in October of 2022.[102] This decision will be one of the most important in recent years and *the* most important when it comes to the future of abortion rights in this country. The recent political climate tells us that no matter the decision made by the Court, the public will certainly make their voices heard, as they have already. The Court's decision is unknown but it is known that *Dobbs v. Jackson* will have a lasting impact on women's reproductive freedom.

---

[99] Id.

[100] Id.

[101] Id.

[102] Andrew Hamm, Dobbs v. Jackson Women's Health Organization SCOTUSblog, https://www.scotusblog.com/case-files/cases/dobbs-v-jackson-womens-health-organization/ (last visited Feb 27, 2022).

RELIGIOUS FREEDOM, LGBTQ AMERICANS, & CIVIL RIGHTS

BY ERIC O'DRISCOLL

INTRODUCTION

The First Amendment states, "Congress shall make no law respecting an establishment of religion, or prohibiting the free exercise thereof..." Composed of the *Establishment Clause* and *Free Exercise Clause*, the First Amendment is the basis for freedom of religion protections in the United States. These rights have remained a cornerstone of American society for centuries. Since 1804, the U.S. Supreme Court has delivered over 870 rulings involving First Amendment freedoms, oftentimes considering other constitutional issues in the process. For example, the Supreme Court has ruled extensively on the intersection between education and the First Amendment's Free Exercise Clause. In *Wisconsin v. Yoder* (1972), the court ruled that a Wisconsin state law requiring that all children attend school until the age of 16 was superseded by the First Amendment rights of Amish parents who wished to adhere to the religious tradition of ending formal education after the eighth grade.[103] The intersection between religious freedom and educational law is evident in this case and many more.

In more recent years, the civil rights of LGBTQ Americans have emerged as a particularly salient issue. Most people will recollect the decision in *Obergefell v. Hodges* (2015), which guaranteed the right to marry for all same-sex couples.[104] However, there remains a struggle between religious groups and the LGBTQ community. This tension has once again reached the Supreme Court in *Fulton v. City of Philadelphia* (2021), in which the Catholic Social Services foster care agency was barred from placing children in foster homes by the City of Philadelphia due to their objection to the city's nondiscrimination requirement which would require them to accept same-sex couples as foster parents.[105] In deciding this case, the Supreme Court relied on decades worth of both legislative and legal precedent.

EMPLOYMENT DIVISION V. SMITH
(1990)

In 1990, the Supreme Court heard the case of *Employment Division, Department of Human Resources of Oregon v. Smith.*[106] The case concerns two employees of a private drug rehabilitation agency who were fired for ingesting peyote–a powerful hallucinogen. They did so as a part of a religious ceremony in accordance with

---

[103] Wisconsin v. Yoder, 406 U.S. 205 (1972)
[104] Obergefell v. Hodges, 576 U.S. 644 (2015)
[105] Fulton v. City of Philadelphia, 593 U.S. __ (2021)
[106] Employment Division, Department of Human Resources of Oregon v. Smith, 494 U.S. 872 (1990)

the Native American Church. Following their termination, both employees filed for unemployment benefits but were denied due to their termination officially resulting from work-related misconduct.[107] At the state level, the primary question of the case was whether or not the use of illegal drugs for sacramental or religious purposes violated Oregon's state drug laws. However, the U.S. Supreme Court stated that the primary concern of the case was regarding whether the Free Exercise Clause of the First Amendment permitted the State of Oregon to criminalize religiously inspired peyote use.[108] The Court ultimately ruled in favor of the Employment Division of Oregon.

Justice Antonin Scalia authored the majority opinion for the court, asserting that there have been two types of free exercise cases presented before the Court: *hybrid* and *pure*. Hybrid cases are those which concern both a constitutional right and another unique right.[109] For example, in *Wisconsin v. Yoder* (1972), the court affirmed the rights of Amish parents to dictate the duration of their children's schooling due to the overlapping nature of both parental rights and First Amendment rights.[110] In these hybrid cases, the Supreme Court uses the *strict scrutiny standard*, in which the state must show that it has a compelling governmental interest and uses the least restrictive means of fulfilling that interest. Conversely, pure cases are those where the Court uses a *valid secular policy test* in which the state must only prove that a law has a legitimate governmental

---

[107] Id.

[108] Id.

[109] Id.

[110] Wisconsin v. Yoder, 406 U.S. 205 (1972)

interest and is neutrally applied.[111] Scalia argued that this was a purely religious case, and that combating a national drug problem was a legitimate governmental interest that was applied neutrally by the law to all citizens of Oregon.[112]

As a result, Scalia revolutionized First Amendment interpretation with his majority opinion. His new standard required only that laws had a clear purpose and did not explicitly discriminate on the basis of religion. So long as a law met these loose standards, any objections to that law on the basis of First Amendment rights would be voided. This shift in standard seriously threatened the interests of religious minorities, whose specific concerns were not given regular attention by federal or state governments.

THE RELIGIOUS FREEDOM RESTORATION ACT

In response to the revolutionary decision in *Employment Division v. Smith*, Congress passed the Religious Freedoms Restoration Act (RFRA) in 1993, almost unanimously. The RFRA was signed into law with the intention of prohibiting the federal government from excessively burdening a person's exercise of religion. In order to do so, the RFRA reinstated a guiding strict scrutiny standard for courts to use when hearing cases

---

[111] John R. Hermann, *Employment Division, Department of Human Resources of Oregon v. Smith (1990)*, The First Amendment Encyclopedia (April 2, 2022) https://www.mtsu.edu/first-amendment/article/364/employment-division-department-of-human-resources-of-oregon-v-smith
[112] Employment Division, Department of Human Resources of Oregon v. Smith, 494 U.S. 872 (1990)

concerning the First Amendment.[113] Again, this test asserts that the federal government may not burden or restrict a person's exercise of religion unless it demonstrates that the burden or restriction furthers a compelling government interest and is done through the least restrictive means, essentially overriding Scalia's opinion in *Employment Division v. Smith.*

CITY OF BOERNE
V. FLORES (1997)

Prior to the 1993 federal RFRA, multiple states had already passed their own statewide Religious Freedom Restoration Acts. Presently, 23 states have their own state RFRA.[114] However, there is an important distinction between these state laws, and the applicability of the federal RFRA under the 14th Amendment. The Equal Protection Clause of the 14th Amendment was ratified in 1868, in part to overrule *Dredd Scott v. Sandford* (1857) – which determined that African Americans were not citizens of the United States – but also to extend all constitutional rights to state citizens and ensure that no state enacts legislation drawing distinctions between groups of people.

In 1996, San Antonio zoning authorities denied the Archbishop of San Antonio a permit to expand his church in Boerne, Texas, because the church was

---

[113] The Religious Freedom Restoration Act of 1993, 42 U.S.C. § 2000bb - 42 U.S.C. § 2000bb-4
[114] Jonathan Griffin, *Religious Freedom Restoration Acts,* National Conference of State Legislatures, Vol. 23, No. 17 (Feb. 22, 2022)
https://www.ncsl.org/research/civil-and-criminal-justice/religious-freedom-restoration-acts

claimed to be located within a historic preservation
district. This meant that any new construction within the
bounds of this district was forbidden.[115] Seeing as the
RFRA would have protected the church's expansion, the
City of Boerne claimed the RFRA was unconstitutional
in that its federal authority superseded the local
preservation ordinance. The case of *City of Boerne v.
Flores* (1997) was granted certiorari by the Supreme
Court in 1997 to determine whether the RFRA was an
overstep of the federal government's authority under the
14th Amendment. The Court ultimately ruled in favor of
the City of Boerne, citing that the application of the
RFRA to preempt local construction ordinances was
unconstitutional.[116] Specifically, the federal RFRA could
not be extended to the states. While many states drafted
and passed their own Religious Freedom Restoration
bills in the years following this decision, it significantly
restricted the federal government's authority to control
state and local governments in the name of religious
freedom.[117]

BURWELL V. HOBBY LOBBY (2014)

The Religious Freedom Restoration Act was again called
into question in 2014, when the Supreme Court heard the
case of *Burwell v. Hobby Lobby Stores*. Hobby Lobby
Stores owners sought to operate their business under the
guidance of the Christian faith, meaning that they were
opposed to the use of contraception.[118] This directly
conflicted with the Affordable Care Act provision that
employment-based group healthcare plans must provide

---

[115] City of Boerne v. Flores, 521 U.S. 507 (1997)
[116] Id.
[117] Id.
[118] Burwell v. Hobby Lobby Stores, 573 U.S. 682 (2014)

FDA-approved contraceptive methods.[119] In 2012, the owners of Hobby Lobby Stores sued the Secretary of Health and Human Services, challenging the constitutionality of the contraception requirement by claiming that it violated the Free Exercise Clause of the First Amendment, as well as the Religious Freedoms Restoration Act. The court ultimately ruled that the RFRA was federally enforceable unto private businesses, and therefore private corporations maintained the right to deny providing contraceptives to their employees as a part of their healthcare coverage.[120] This affirmed the federal strength of the RFRA and its applicability regarding the private sector.

FULTON V. CITY OF PHILADELPHIA (2021)

The aforementioned cases present a clear tension between religious freedom and different pieces of local, state, and federal legislation. However, most cases concerning religious freedom in relation to LGBTQ civil rights – with the exception of *Obergefell v. Hodges* (2015) – have emerged from conflicts between individuals and private entities. For example, in *Masterpiece Cakeshop, Ltd. v. Colorado Civil Rights Commission* (2018) the Supreme Court determined that a Christian bakery could deny its services to a same-sex couple who wanted to purchase a wedding cake.[121] Similarly, in *Boy Scouts of America v. Dale* (1996), the court affirmed that a private organization, in this case the

---

[119] Patient Protection and Affordable Care Act of 2010, 42 U.S.C. § 18001

[120] Burwell v. Hobby Lobby Stores, 573 U.S. 682 (2014)

[121] Masterpiece Cakeshop, Ltd. v. Colorado Civil Rights Commission, 584 U.S. __ (2018)

Boy Scouts, could bar homosexuals from serving in leadership positions in accordance with their right to freedom of association, as protected under the First Amendment.[122]

However, *Fulton v. City of Philadelphia* (2021) addresses the contractual relationship between state actors and private entities.[123] Philadelphia's foster care system consists of a series of contracts between the City and private foster care agencies, who are responsible for placing children with families. Catholic Social Services (CSS) has contracted with the City of Philadelphia to provide foster care services for over 50 years, and holds the religious belief that marriage is intended to exist exclusively between one man and one woman. As a result, CSS will not provide foster services to unmarried couples or same-sex couples. Other private foster agencies in Philadelphia will work with same-sex couples, and no same-sex couple has ever attempted to receive services from CSS.[124] However, in 2018 the City informed CSS that it needed to agree to certify same-sex couples, or they would lose their contract with the city due to a violation of a non-discrimination provision in the agency's contract with the City.[125] CSS filed against Philadelphia on the grounds that the City's actions violated the Free Exercise and Free Speech Clauses of the First Amendment. In doing so, they posed the question of whether or not the government violated the First Amendment by refusing to contract with CSS due to their refusal to certify same-sex couples as foster

---

[122] Boy Scouts of America v. Dale, 530 U.S. 640 (2000)
[123] Fulton v. City of Philadelphia, 593 U.S. __ (2021)
[124] Fulton v. City of Philadelphia, 593 U.S. __ (2021)
[125] Id.

parents.[126] Additionally, the Court needed to revisit, and potentially revise, the decision in *Employment Division v. Smith* (1990).

Ultimately, the Court ruled unanimously in favor of CSS, stating that the refusal of Philadelphia to enter into a contract with CSS unless they agreed to certify same-sex couples as foster parents violates the Free Exercise Clause.[127] Chief Justice John Roberts authored the majority opinion of the Court, citing that the City of Philadelphia's refusal to contract with CSS burdened the religious institution's ability to exercise its mission, and would have forced them to violate their religious beliefs.[128] The Court determined that the Philadelphia law was not neutrally applicable.[129] Therefore, it did not even meet the standard set in *Employment Division v. Smith*, meaning the anti-discrimination requirement from the City of Philadelphia would be subject to strict scrutiny.[130] This meant that the government would need to demonstrate that the standard is necessary for a compelling government interest. The Court noted that the failure to make a religious exemption from the non-discrimination policy serves no government interest, and therefore violates the First Amendment.[131]

CONCLUSION

---

[126] Id.
[127] Id.
[128] Id.
[129] Id.
[130] Employment Division, Department of Human Resources of Oregon v. Smith, 494 U.S. 872 (1990)
[131] Fulton v. City of Philadelphia, 593 U.S. __ (2021)

The decision in *Fulton v. City of Philadelphia* may prove to be a significant precedent to future First Amendment cases. In its decision, the Court bypassed the loose scrutiny standards set by Justice Scalia in *Employment Division v. Smith,* opting to examine the case with a strict scrutiny test. Ultimately, it was the controversial decision in *Smith* that led to the hugely bipartisan Religious Freedom Restoration Act in 1993.[132] Of course, this act was mitigated by *City of Boerne v. Flores* (1997).[133] Still, it demonstrated that the government cannot interject and propose which ideological framework is morally correct. In other words, the fractured RFRA and decisions in *Fulton* and *Burwell* have consistently reaffirmed the First Amendment protections to freedom of religion, even if they are in direct conflict with the civil rights of LGBTQ Americans.

---

[132] Employment Division, Department of Human Resources of Oregon v. Smith, 494 U.S. 872 (1990)
[133] City of Boerne v. Flores, 521 U.S. 507 (1997)

FEDERAL APPROACHES TO FOSTER CARE: FAMILY UNITY AT THE EXPENSE OF IMMEDIATE NEEDS

BY MORGAN HARRIS

INTRODUCTION

As of 2020, there were over 400,000 children in foster care systems in the United States according to the U.S. Department of Health and Human Services Children's Bureau.[134] A 2019 Jama Pediatrics study found that the number of foster children had more than doubled from 2000 to 2017, primarily due to parental drug abuse due to the opioid epidemic.[135] Economic insecurity, alternative forms of drug abuse, and the mental health

---

[134] Administration for Children and Families, Administration on Children, Youth and Families, Children's Bureau, Adoption and Foster Care Analysis and Reporting System (2020).

[135] Meinhofer A, Angleró-Díaz Y. Trends in Foster Care Entry Among Children Removed From Their Homes Because of Parental Drug Use, 2000 to 2017. *JAMA Pediatr.* 2019;173(9):881–883. doi:10.1001/jamapediatrics.2019.1738

impact of the COVID-19 pandemic have also been contributing factors toward the recent spike in foster care entries.[136]

Foster care has historically been under state jurisdiction in the United States, with increased federal involvement over time. As time has progressed, the federal government has shifted from little involvement, simply requiring that states have foster care systems established, to a proactive approach that addresses the root causes of displacement. However, despite growth in the federal oversight of foster care, the federal government has taken an inconsistent approach requiring states to implement programs with little structure or support. By requiring that states have goals, such as family reunification, yet lacking federal support, the federal government prevents states from meeting the needs of those involved in foster systems at all levels.

HISTORY OF FEDERAL INVOLVEMENT IN FOSTER CARE

Federal involvement in state foster care began as a way to enforce the existence of foster care programs. Congress authorized the first grants to states to fund child welfare services under the Social Security Act of 1935.[137] Although these first grants were small, they allowed some states to establish foster care and child

---

[136] Char Adams, Foster Care Crisis: More kids are entering, but fewer families are willing to take them in NBCNews.com (2020), https://www.nbcnews.com/news/nbcblk/foster-care-crisis-more-kids-are-entering-fewer-families-are-n1252450 (last visited Feb 28, 2022).
[137] The Social Security Act of 1935, H.R. 7620 §§ 74-271

welfare programs for the first time.[138] Congress later amended the act in 1962 to require that states report families whose children were 'candidates for removal' (i.e., living in unsuitable conditions) to the court system.[139] A further amendment in 1967 required all states to implement foster care programs.[140] These developments marked the first acts of pressure for state action toward foster care by the federal government.

Historically, the federal government has applied pressure onto states to implement foster care efforts without providing the long term support necessary to see lasting change. States can apply for individual grants from federal supplemental programs such as the John H. Chafee Foster Care Independence Program. This supports youth currently and formerly in foster care with services including training and education to aid in transitioning to adulthood. While the program makes support services possible, they are not automatically provided.

The federal emphasis on family reunification was first apparent in the 1980 Adoption Assistance and Child Welfare Act (AACWA). Created in response to concerns that foster children were staying in the system too long, the AACWA required that states make "reasonable efforts" to reunite children with their families through both preventative and reunification services.[141]

---

[138] Kasia O'Neill Murray & Sarah Gesiriech, A Brief Legislative History of the Child Welfare System (2004).
[139] The Public Welfare Amendments of 1962 §§ 87-543.
[140] Social Security Amendments of 1967 H.R. 12080, 1 amend. 3.
[141] 1980 Adoption Assistance and Child Welfare Act H.R. 3434, 4 §§ 96-900.

The number of children in the foster system declined as a result of AACWA until various factors like the AIDS epidemic and higher incarceration rates caused an increase in cases in the mid-1980s.[142] As a result of this increase as well as lingering concerns about family reunification efforts, Congress established the 1993 Family Preservation and Family Support Services Program (FPFSSP), giving states funding to implement services that prevent child abuse, neglect, and initial foster system entries.[143] The FPFSSP marks the federal advocacy for a proactive foster care approach with prevention and family reunification.

FAMILY FIRST PREVENTION CARE ACT

One of the most recent federal developments in foster care was the Family First Prevention Services Act (FFPSA) of 2017, an act signed under the Trump administration that prioritizes keeping children with their biological families.[144] The FFPSA continued the federal government's transition from a reactive to proactive foster care approach. Before the act, the federal government reimbursed states for foster care spending.[145] Now, the FFPSA has established measures preventing initial foster care entry and funding preventative resources like mental health services, substance abuse treatment, and in-home parenting support for families of children at risk of entering the foster system.[146]

---

[142] Id. note 5.
[143] The Social Security Act of 1993, IV-B.
[144] Family First Prevention Services Act of 2017 H.R. 1982 §§ 115-123.
[145] Id. note 5.
[146] Id. note 11.

While the federal government has invested in preventative care measures, this support may be insufficient for some families due to its lack of long term care. The FFPSA provides *up to* twelve months of preventative care for families of children at risk of entering foster care.[147] However, the State Policy Advocacy and Reform Center's Adoption and Foster Care Analysis and Reporting System found that reunification in less than twelve months is more likely to result in reentry into foster care.[148] Without long-term investments in aiding the root causes that push children into the foster system, many families' needs may not be met. Opioid addictions, which are a main cause of child entrance into foster care, typically take a minimum of twelve months to treat.[149] Families struggling with mental illnesses may also struggle to remain fit to parent once they are left without care and left to deal with their illness alone.

One way the Family First Prevention Services Act attempts to avoid family separation is by placing limits on group homes, temporary housing placements similar to orphanages, in which foster children without a foster parent are placed. FFPSA caps federal funding for group homes and limits the length of time children are allowed to stay in group homes, limiting reimbursement to states

---

[147] Id. note 11.

[148] John Sciamanna, Reunification of Foster Children with their Families: The First Permanency Outcome (2013).

[149] National Institute of Health, Principles of Drug Addiction Treatment: A Research-Based Guide. How long does drug addiction treatment usually last? (2018), https://nida.nih.gov/publications/principles-drug-addiction-treatment-research-based-guide-third-edition/frequently-asked-questions/how-long-does-drug-addiction-treatment-usually-last.

to only two weeks of group home care per child.[150] The act presumes that by cutting off resources to group homes, states will be forced to prioritize family unification over temporary placement.

Research shows that children are better off in a family environment than in congregate living.[151] However, the FFPSA's two-week cut off for federal funding for a child's group home stay places a burden on foster children whose families have not yet benefited from preventative care. This provision causes states to move children between temporary foster homes and group homes potentially every two weeks, or whenever the state runs out of its own funding beyond federal support.[152] States who can not make the rapid move away from group home dependency have the option to waive this requirement, continuing to receive funding beyond two weeks.[153] However, states who choose this option waive the preventative funding that the FFPSA provides.[154] Without preventative care funding, states lack the support to move children out of group homes. The FFPSA pressures states to push children in foster children into one extreme or the other, either living with their families or in an unstable environment, moving between temporary foster home placements and group homes.

---

[150] Id. note 11

[151] Meghan McCann, The Child Welfare Placement Continuum: What's Best for Children? The Child Welfare Placement Continuum: What's best for children? (2019), https://www.ncsl.org/research/human-services/the-child-welfare-placement-continuum-what-s-best-for-children.aspx

[152] Id. note 11

[153] Id. note 11

[154] Id. note 11

The hyper focus on family reunification under FFPSA can foster dangerous environments for some children. In early 2000, two-year-old Brianna Blackmond was beaten and killed only two weeks after being moved by DC courts from her foster home into the care of her mother, who had a history of neglect.[155] While some states may develop comprehensive programs with federal funding, there is no uniform approach among states because the federal government asks states to develop their own independent solutions. Therefore, while some states will develop programs that effectively place children in the best placements, others are at risk of perpetuating neglect and abuse due to the federal pressure of family unification.

The U.S. Department of Health and Human Services Children's Bureau states that the goal of the FFPSA is, "to avoid that trauma that results when children are placed in out-of-home care."[156] While not ideal, congregate care, like group homes, is necessary for some children. Rather than improving group homes and congregate living situations to avoid the trauma children experience in them, the FFPSA disregards congregate living overall.

The Family First Prevention Services Act requires that states have certain goals in their foster care efforts, but

---

[155] Lost Children: Brianna Blackmond, The Washington Post (2000),
https://www.washingtonpost.com/wp-srv/photo/metro/lost_chi ldren/blackmond.htm (last visited Feb 28, 2022).

[156] Administration for Children and Families, Child Welfare Information Gateway (2020),
https://www.childwelfare.gov/topics/systemwide/laws-policies /federal/family-first/#:~:text=1892 (last visited 2022).

fails to provide effective, uniform instruction on how to reach those goals. For instance, the act requires that states come up with a plan to prevent children from dying of abuse and neglect.[157] While states can have unique reasons behind their foster care population based on factors such as geographic location that correlate with varying drug abuse and poverty rates, the non-uniform approach gives unclear work to the states and makes it difficult to study the impacts of the FFPSA.

CONCLUSION

The federal approach to foster care has progressed in a direction that recognizes the importance of targeting root causes, preventing children from ever entering the foster system in the first place. However, their preventative approach neglects the immediate needs of many children in the foster care system who rely on resources like congregate care. Additionally, the federal government relies heavily on the states to develop effective solutions to problems in foster care without providing assistance to create these programs. A greater investment in preventative solutions as well as improvements to the current systems that children realistically deal with could decrease foster care entries and improve the experience of children in foster care.

---

[157] Id. note 11

THE AMERICAN UNIVERSITY
UNDERGRADUATE LAW JOURNAL

AU UNDERGRAD
LAW JOURNAL

CONSTITUTIONAL

LAW

COLUMN

NDAS VS. FREEDOM OF SPEECH

BY JENNA BOLONIK

INTRODUCTION

There are no trade-offs within the Constitution; there are rights guaranteed unequivocally to all persons inhabiting the land of the United States. Controversy surrounding the free speech clause of the First Amendment typically includes talk of hate speech, defamatory rhetoric, and obscenities. The sheer purpose of the First Amendment was to limit the power of the government, essentially giving power to the people. Do attempts by government officials to silence less powerful voices using tools like Non-Disclosure Agreements (NDAs) (contracts that prevent sensitive information from being shared), threaten democratic values and guard corruption?[158]

HISTORICAL BACKGROUND

---

[158] Alexandra Twin, Non-Disclosure Agreement (NDA), *Investopedia*, (2021), https://www.investopedia.com/terms/n/nda.asp

The Supreme Court case *Cohen v. Cowles Media Co.* was the primitive display of the Court's approach to private contracts like NDAs.[159] In Minnesota's 1982 gubernatorial race, Dan Cohen, an associate of Republican candidate Wheelock Whitney, sought out reporters from the *Pioneer Press* and *Star Tribune* to provide information on the opposing party's campaign.[160] Cohen agreed to provide documentation so long as "his identity [remains] confidential."[161] Disregarding this condition, the reporters identified Cohen as the source in the publication. This led to him getting fired, so Cohen sued *Cowles Media Co.* for breach of contract.[162] The Supreme Court held that "[the] media could be sued for breach of contract for divulging the identity of a confidential source."[163] This was a private matter of promissory estoppel – "the doctrine that a party may recover on the basis of a promise made when the party's reliance on that promise was reasonable, and the party attempting to recover detrimentally relied on the promise."[164] The Minnesota Supreme Court had to decide if state action was

---

[159] Cohen, 501 U.S. 663

[160] Abigail Stephens, Contracting Away the First Amendment?: When Courts Should Intervene in Nondisclosure Agreements, 28 Wm. & Mary Bill Rts. J. 541 (2019), https://scholarship.law.wm.edu/wmborj/vol28/iss2/12

[161] Id.

[162] Id.

[163] Patrick M. Garry, *Cohen v. Cowles Media Co.* (1991), The First Amendment Encyclopedia, https://www.mtsu.edu/first-amendment/article/741/cohen-v-cowles-media-co

[164] Promissory Estoppel, Legal Information Institute https://www.law.cornell.edu/wex/promissory_estoppel#:~:text=Within%20contract%20law%2C%20promissory%20estoppel,detrimentally%20relied%20on%20the%20promise.

involved.[165] Precedent compelled the conclusion that there was state action involved, thus triggering the First Amendment.[166]

If you are wondering why the First Amendment was triggered, as it was supposed to protect journalists' rights to divulge sources, you aren't alone. The trigger was "pulled" because the First Amendment was allowing "newspapers to breach the promises their reporters made to their sources."[167] Promissory estoppel steps in here because Cohen was able to recover on the basis that he was guaranteed his identity would remain confidential (the "promise"), and he relied on the promise.

The law in Minnesota requires promises to be kept in this sense, and that any restrictions placed on truthful publications are "self-imposed."[168] This was interpreted to mean that the Court takes a "hands-off" approach with regard to NDAs.[169] There are two main reasons for this approach: (1) "citizens in a free society should be able to freely enter into agreements of their choosing, generally unfettered by court interference" and (2) the efficiency of a judicial system.[170] The concern in the first reason is that the Court's interference in NDAs would infringe on private parties' rights; the concern in the second reason is that the courts would become severely overwhelmed in deciding private party matters.

---

[165] Cohen, 501 U.S. 668
[166] Id.
[167] Jerome A. Barron, Cohen v. Cowles Media and its Significance for First Amendment Law and Journalism, 3 Wm. & Mary Bill Rts. J. 419 (1994), https://scholarship.law.wm.edu/wmborj/vol3/ iss2/3
[168] Cohen, 501 U.S. 671
[169] Id. per 2
[170] Id.

VALIDITY OF NDAS IN THE PUBLIC SECTOR

The two concerns listed above are clearly valid when pertaining to private party matters. The hiccup arises when we enter the realm of the public sector. Former President Donald J. Trump's administration asked senior White House staff members to sign NDAs "vowing not to reveal confidential information and exposing them to damages for any violation."[171] The penalty for breach of contract was initially set at $10 million, but it was purportedly lowered in the final version.[172] This raised controversy because this sum was "payable to the federal government, for each and any unauthorized revelation of "confidential" information."[173] The NDA also outlined restrictions for White House aides both during their tenure and "at all times thereafter."[174] This is a manipulation tactic that uses substantial monetary penalties that are unaffordable to the average person to intimidate government employees into being complacent.

The courts have previously placed a limit on free speech that says government employees may be fired for saying things that interfere with their employers' efficiency.[175]

---

[171] Ruth Marcus, *Opinion: Trump had senior staff sign nondisclosure agreements. They're supposed to last beyond his presidency,* The Washington Post, March 28, 2018, https://www.washingtonpost.com/opinions/trumps-nondisclos ure-agreements-came-with-him-to-the-white-house/2018/03/1 8/226f4522-29ee-11e8-b79d-f3d931db7f68_story.html
[172] Id.
[173] Id.
[174] Id.
[175]Permissible restrictions on expression Encyclopædia Britannica,

For this reason, the Supreme Court "upheld a ban on broadcasting vulgar words" in *FCC v. Pacifica Foundation* (1978).[176]

The additional limitation by the Trump administration is an overreach because it is already prohibited for White House employees to reveal classified information or attorney-client privilege.[177] So, when a carefully worded and binding contract is imposed as an additional privacy restriction for non-classified information, it raises a red flag. For many years, the courts have ruled that the government cannot censor unclassified material.[178] Scholars feel that an economic penalty is an attempt to limit free speech, which questions the constitutionality of NDAs in government.[179]

The system of checks and balances in the United States is responsible for ensuring that no branch of government abuses its power; in this case, the judicial branch has a responsibility to check the power of the executive. By not doing so and using a hands-off approach, it is arguable that the White House employees had their rights infringed upon. In order to check the president's power, the courts should nullify an NDA that would

---

https://www.britannica.com/topic/First-Amendment/Permissible-restrictions-on-expression
[176] Id.
[177] Id.
[178] Zaid, Mark S. "Perspective | The Constitution Won't Let Trump Silence White House Aides." The Washington Post. WP Company, August 14, 2018. https://www.washingtonpost.com/news/posteverything/wp/2018/08/14/the-constitution-wont-let-trump-silence-white-house-aides/.
[179] Id.

censor the free speech of White House officials.[180] The courts' hands-off approach is insufficient. White House officials are employees of the federal government, not the former president himself. This approach arguably aids the violation of Constitutional rights.

DUTY TO THE PEOPLE

The people of the United States pay the salaries of White House staff members, not the president. The agency theory in business provides that corporations are agents of their shareholders; similarly, public officials are agents of the people they serve. Therefore, they have a duty of transparency. Freedom of speech is necessary to successfully fulfill this duty because effective communication of discrepancies is integral between the public service and the public. Not only is former President Trump's attempt to silence White House staff an effort at infringing upon their Constitutional rights, it also impedes transparency. The Transparency and Government Accountability Act asserts that the government "has a duty to affirmatively disclose certain information, in a timely manner, and to shift the burden from citizens and journalists to the state."[181] When

---

[180] Scott Horsley, *Sworn To Secrecy: Trump's History Of Using Nondisclosure Agreements*, NPR, March 19, 2018, https://www.npr.org/2018/03/19/595025070/sworn-to-secrecy-trumps-history-of-using-nondisclosure-agreements
[181] *Transparency and Government Accountability Act,* American Legislative Exchange Council, https://alec.org/model-policy/transparency-and-government-ac countability-act/#:~:text=%E2%80%9CTransparency%E2%80 %9D%20is%20government's%20obligation%20to,conduct%2 0of%20the%20people's%20business.

powerful people initiate NDAs intending to silence their subordinates, they should be held accountable.

SHELBY COUNTY v. HOLDER: THE DESTRUCTION OF AMERICA'S MOST FUNDAMENTAL RIGHT

BY BEN PARSONS

INTRODUCTION

In 20, the five conservative Justices of the Supreme Court of the United States shocked many legal observers by overturning the rulings of both the lower district and appeals courts by declaring Section 4 of the Voting Rights Act unconstitutional. In there ruling, the Supreme Court overturned nearly 50 years of legal precedent established in *South Carolina v. Katzenbach* and declared that, since voting conditions have changed significantly enough since 1965, the formula used to determine whether a voting law was discriminatory is no longer necessary and is, rather, an unconstitutional overreach of Congress' power. By doing so, the conservative majority on the Supreme Court has wiped out years of progress in ending voter discrimination and has reopened the door for enacting restrictive voting laws.

THE VOTING RIGHTS ACT:
A QUICK EXPLANATION AND LEGISLATIVE HISTORY

Five years following the end of the American Civil War, Congress passed the Fifteenth Amendment to the Constitution, establishing that "the right of citizens of the United States to vote shall not be denied or abridged by the United States or by any State on account of race, color, or previous condition of servitude".[182] Despite the seemingly clear language, African Americans in the United States still faced major obstacles in actually practicing their right to vote. In the midst of the civil rights movement, President Lyndon B. Johnson signed into law the Voting Rights Act of 1965 to combat these obstacles.[183]

While the Voting Rights Act consists of a number of sections, the most important are Sections 2, 4 and 5. Section 2 makes it illegal to "deny or abridge the right of any citizen of the United States to vote on account of race or color".[184] Section 5 addressed the reality that discriminatory voting practices often was more prevalent in certain areas of the country. It created a rule establishing that certain jurisdictions (states and some counties) must be "covered" by the US Department of Justice. These "covered" jurisdictions were required by

---

[182] U.S. Const. amend. XV, § 1.

[183] *Congress and the Voting Rights Act of 1965*, National Archives (Oct. 2022), https://www.archives.gov/legislative/features/voting-rights-1965.

[184] *Transcript of Voting Rights Act (1954),* Our Documents (2022), https://www.ourdocuments.gov/doc.php?flash=false&doc=100&page=transcript.

law to submit any changes to voting laws to either the US District Court for the District of Columbia or to the US Attorney General to ensure the law "does not have the purpose and will not have the effect of denying or abridging the right to vote on account of race or color".[185] Section 4, particularly section 4(b), established the "clearance formula" that determined which jurisdictions require "preclearance" by the Department of Justice for changes to voting laws.[186]

Importantly, while some parts of the Voting Rights Act were intended to last indefinitely, other parts required reauthorization after a number of years. In the initial iteration of the legislation in 1965, Congress authorized Section 4(b) for only five years, but in 1970, Congress reauthorized Section 4(b) for another five years.[187] This occurred a total of five times, each time with vast majorities in Congress. Most recently, in 2006, reauthorization of Section 4(b) for another 25 years passed the US House of Representatives by a vote of 390-33,[188] and the US Senate by a vote of 98-0.[189] It was signed by President George W. Bush a mere week later.[190]

---

[185] Ibid.
[186] Ibid.
[187] *PUBLIC LAW 91-383 - Aug. 18 1970*, Gov Info (2022), https://www.govinfo.gov/content/pkg/STATUTE-84/pdf/STATUTE-84-Pg825.pdf.
[188] *House Vote #374 in 2006 (109th Congress)*, Govtrack (2022), https://www.govtrack.us/congress/votes/109-2006/h374.
[189] Ibid.
[190] *H.R. 9 (109th)*, Govtrack (2022), https://www.govtrack.us/congress/bills/109/hr9.

LEGAL CHALLENGES AND *SHELBY COUNTY*: DESTROYING PRECEDENT BASED OFF MOOD

While the Voting Rights Act of 1965 seems relatively non-divisive when looking at the margins the law was reauthorized at, the Voting Rights Act represented both a massive overhaul of the US election system and the first federal voting law. Within five months of its enactment, the first legal challenge to the legislation came in the form of *South Carolina v. Katzenbach*. South Carolina appealed directly to the Supreme Court, arguing the federal government, among other things, was "unconstitutionally encroaching on States' rights" to administer elections.[191]

After hearing these arguments, the Supreme Court affirmed the legality of the Voting Rights Act. By an 8-1 decision, the court affirmed Section 5's "preclearance" requirement, noting that Congress "is free to use whatever means are appropriate to carry out the objects of the Constitution".[192] The court also upheld the "coverage formula" of Section 4(b) stating that the formula is "rational" in its birth and in its targeting certain geographic areas and that its burden of proof is not unreasonable.[193] In denying every argument made by South Carolina, the Warren Court set the precedent that both the concept of preclearance and the coverage formula was completely permissible within Congress' legislative power. These were once again upheld in

---

[191] <u>South Carolina v. Katzenbach</u>, 383 U.S. 301 (1966).
[192] Ibid.
[193] Ibid.

Georgia v. US (1973),[194] *City of Rome v. US* (1980),[195] and in *Georgia v. Ashcroft* (2003).[196]

Despite these affirmations, in 2013, John Roberts' majority opinion in *Shelby County v. Holder* overturned years of precedent, finding that the clearance formula in Section 4(b) unconstitutional. While it is true that just because something is precedent does not mean that it is constitutionally valid, in this opinion Roberts makes no argument that the precedent was wrong. In fact, Roberts even goes as far as to say that the court in *South Carolina v. Katzenbach* was "justified" in its decision.[197] In fact, Roberts praises the Voting Rights Act saying that "there is no doubt that these improvements are in large part because of the Voting Rights Act".[198] Yet, Roberts goes on to say that while Section 4(b) of the Voting Rights Act was correct in addressing voting discrimination in 1966 it "no longer does so".[199] Roberts even argues that these conclusions are not the courts alone pointing to the 2006 reauthorization of the Voting Rights Act and quoting "[s]ignificant progress has been made in eliminating first-generation barriers experienced by minority voters, including increased numbers of registered minority voters, minority voter turnout, and minority representation in Congress, State legislatures, and local elected offices".[200] Roberts' entire argument rests on the principle that if there was still significant voter discrimination today, Section 4(b) would be

---

[194] Georgia v US, 411 U.S. 526 (1973).
[195] City of Rome v US, 446 U.S. 156 (1980).
[196] Georgia v Ashcroft, 539 U.S. 461 (2003).
[197] Shelby County v. Holder, 570 U.S. 529 (2013).
[198] Ibid.
[199] Ibid.
[200] Ibid.

constitutional - but this voting discrimination does not exist.

Richly, in quoting Congress to make this point, Roberts conveniently leaves out the next few sentences. The reauthorization goes on to say "however, vestiges of discrimination in voting continue to exist as demonstrated by second generation barriers constructed to prevent minority voters from fully participating in the electoral process".[201] It then provides nearly three pages of evidence that voter discrimination is still alive and well in this country, and that only the coverage formula of the Voting Rights Act can prevent it.

Unfortunately, Congress is not the only one to identify voter discrimination. According to the Brennan Center For Justice, since 2010 "25 states have put in place new restrictions".[202] The vast majority of these restrictions have been enacted after *Shelby County v. Holder* and, as the US Commission On Civil Rights notes, this is likely due to the fact that many of these voting restrictions would have been found too restrictive under the Voting Rights Act.[203] While some of these bills have been "facially neutral" some have had a clearly discriminatory intent. While the legislation didn't end up being passed,

[201] *Public Law 109-246 - 109th Congress*, Gov Info (2022), https://www.govinfo.gov/content/pkg/PLAW-109publ246/html/PLAW-109publ246.htm.
[202] *New Voting Restrictions in America*, Brennan Center For Justice (Nov. 19, 2019), https://www.brennancenter.org/our-work/research-reports/new-voting-restrictions-america.
[203] *An Assessment of Minority Voting Rights Access in the United States*, US Commission on Civil Rights (2018), https://www.usccr.gov/files/pubs/2018/Minority_Voting_Access_2018.pdf.

legislation in Georgia was introduced to exclude voting on Sundays - clearly an attempt to limit black worshipers in Georgia from partaking in early voting directly after worship, a practice called "souls to the polls".[204] Other laws across the country focus on limiting the hours and locations of voting places in areas where minority populations live in high concentrations, and others have "purged" voter rolls of "inactive voters", disproportionately impacting minority voters. Even if John Roberts' legal opinion was correct, the premise he bases it off is completely detached from reality

JOHN ROBERTS' LIES

While the opinion that if voter discrimination was not occurring, Section 4(b) would be an unconstitutional overreach is weak, one might be able to make an argument that Section 4(b) is unconstitutional. Yet, John Roberts and the conservative majority on the Supreme Court apply this rational in a time when voter discrimination does still occur. As Justice Ginsburg states in her dissent "throwing out preclearance... is like throwing away your umbrella in a rainstorm because you are not getting wet".[205] Continuing this analogy: not only did John Roberts and the conservative majority in *Shelby County v. Holder* throw away the umbrella, they destroyed it and every other umbrella in the United States while forcing America's voting protections to sit face up at the base of Niagara Falls.

---

[204] *Georgia voting: Fact-checking claims about the new election law*, BBC (Apr.7 2021), https://www.bbc.com/news/world-us-canada-56650565.
[205] Shelby County v. Holder, 570 U.S. 529 (2013).

THE AMERICAN UNIVERSITY
UNDERGRADUATE LAW JOURNAL

AU UNDERGRAD
LAW JOURNAL

CRIMINAL LAW
COLUMN

LEGALIZATION vs. DECRIMINALIZATION OF MARIJUANA IN THE U.S.

BY SHREYA DIWAN

INTRODUCTION

Marijuana is a psychoactive drug and is derived from cannabis- a plant native to Central and South Asia. There is a long history of human use of the drug in these areas where ancient cultures grew the plant to create herbal medicines.[206] The use of the drug in America dates back to colonial times when farmers grew hemp to aid in making clothing, paper, rope, etc. Marijuana use heavily increased in the U.S. in the early 1900s for both recreational and medical purposes, but political and racial factors of that time period led to the heavy criminalization of marijuana. Marijuana has long been considered a "gateway drug", a substance that is thought to pave the way to using more dangerous or harder drugs such as heroin or cocaine. Generally, people who use drugs are labeled as "criminals" or are seen as outcasts

---

[206] National Institute on Drug Abuse, *History of Cannabis, Part 1,* https://archives.drugabuse.gov/blog/post/history-of-cannabis-part-1, (last visited April 5, 2022).

in society. Today, however, new research has decreased the negative stigma against marijuana. The drug is now being recommended to cancer patients to relieve intense nausea caused by chemotherapy. It is also said to relieve migraines and painful symptoms of epilepsy patients.[207] As a result, the U.S. is realizing the benefits associated with the drug and many states have decriminalized or even legalized marijuana. Many jurisdictions are taking a step in a more tolerant direction by loosening harsher penalties for the use and possession of the drug. As of the end of 2021, 18 states have legalized marijuana and eight more are due to vote on its legalization in 2022.[208] Furthermore, there are 27 states in the U.S. that have decriminalized marijuana.[209] These state reforms, superseding the marijuana stigma, may decrease mass incarceration, reduce harmful racial stereotypes associated with the drug, and alter the poor public opinion of drug addiction as a criminal issue.

CRIMINALIZATION OF MARIJUANA

Marijuana was first made illegal in the U.S. through The Marihuana Tax Act of 1937, the first federal law used to criminalize the drug.[210] Congress was able to pass legislation taxing marijuana because the majority of the

---

[207] FDA, *Statement by FDA Commissioner Scott Gottlieb,* https://www.fda.gov/news-events/press-announcements/statement-fda-commissioner-scott-gottlieb-md-importance-conducting-proper-research-prove-safe-and, (last visited April 2, 2022).

[208] Business Insider, *States Where Marijuana,* https://www.businessinsider.com/legal-marijuana-states-2018-1, (last visited April 1, 2022).

[209] National Conference of State Legislatures, *Cannabis Overview,* https://www.ncsl.org/research/civil-and-criminal-justice/marijuana-overview.aspx#:~:text=Twenty%2Dseven%20states%20and%20the,no%20possibility%20of%20jail%20time), (last visited April 1, 2022).

[210] The Marihuana Tax Act of 1937, Pub.L. 75–238, 50 Stat. 551

country saw it as a negative substance. Despite its purported medical benefits, many people changed their attitude towards cannabis partly due to the Mexican immigration to the U.S. at this time. The prejudices and fears Americans had about Mexican immigrants extended to the immigrants' traditional means of intoxication which was smoking marijuana. The act was essentially a nationwide ban on the importation, cultivation, possession, and/or distribution of marijuana. As the years passed, punishments increased if people were caught in possession of the drug, and the start of the War on Drugs in 1971 made these punishments even more severe.[211] This extensive government-led initiative created to stop illegal drug use, possession, and distribution was led by President Richard Nixon. It repealed the Marihuana Tax Act and introduced a more punitive act to replace it. The Controlled Substances Act of 1970 listed marijuana as a Schedule I drug—along with heroin, LSD, and ecstasy.[212] These drugs were recorded as having no medical uses and a high potential for abuse. Suddenly, the use of marijuana was not only illegal but the use of this drug was also seen as equally dangerous to that of substances like heroin. Using schedule I drugs warranted considerably harsher penalties such as spending up to 180 days in jail, a $1,000 fine, or both.[213]

---

[211] NPR, *After 50 Years Of The War On Drugs 'What Good Is It Doing For Us?',*
https://www.npr.org/2021/06/17/1006495476/after-50-years-of-the-war-on-drugs-what-good-is-it-doing-for-us
[212] Controlled Substances Act (CSA), Pub. L. 91-513, 84 Stat. 1236
[213] National Conference of State Legislatures, *Cannabis Overview,*
https://www.ncsl.org/research/civil-and-criminal-justice/marijuana-overview.aspx#:~:text=Twenty%2Dseven%20states%20and%20the,no%20possibility%20of%20jail%20time), (last visited April 1, 2022).

Considering the racial bias and discrimination central to the War on Drugs, Black Americans and people of color (POC) were given exceptionally long sentences if they were caught with small amounts of marijuana. Policies like mandatory minimums enforced a lack of judicial discretion so the nation could arrest as many people as it could for drug-related offenses. The negative effects of the War on Drugs have created lasting social inequality with thousands of minorities behind bars for minor drug-related offenses, especially marijuana-related offenses. Marijuana arrests account for over half of all drug arrests in the United States today and the penalties given to Black people and POC have been grossly disproportionate to that of white people or people of dominant racial groups.[214] Arrest data has revealed significant racial bias in the justice system and minorities continue to be unfairly prosecuted and convicted for minor drug offenses. The harsher punitive measures against the use of marijuana since the 1970s may have prompted biased convictions and contributed to detrimental consequences for those released from prison, resulting in stagnated racism and a bleak standard of mental and physical healthcare for poor Americans.

Prison tends to keep people away from treatment that can help them with addiction meaning that it is unlikely inmates come out of prison healthy. They may be released with the same addiction issue they had when they were locked up. Incarceration also prohibits steady employment leading to financial problems and more triggers that influence addicts to keep using or dealing marijuana. A recent federal survey of high school seniors

---

[214] ACLU, *Marijuana Arrests By The Numbers* (March 4, 2022), https://www.aclu.org/gallery/marijuana-arrests-numbers

seems to indicate that marijuana prohibition does not keep marijuana out of young hands: 85% of students surveyed said it would be "easy" for them to obtain marijuana. Other federal surveys indicate that at least 70 million Americans admitted to having used marijuana (up to one-quarter of all Americans), and that 17 million use it on a monthly basis now.[215] Thus, the criminalization of marijuana has not actually aided in ending drug abuse in America. It has instead created issues for those adjusting to life post-incarceration. Individuals cannot get proper jobs with a drug arrest record and they may still need treatment for addiction making it difficult for them to rejoin society and have equal rights and opportunities as other citizens. The criminalization of marijuana has led to the incarceration of thousands of economically disadvantaged people who will continue to suffer if America does not change its policies to battle drug abuse.

LEGALIZATION vs. DECRIMINALIZATION OF MARIJUANA

As awareness of discrimination in drug arrests and convictions has spread, many states have adopted policies to decriminalize or even legalize marijuana. Decriminalization is the decrease of criminal penalties imposed for using marijuana while the manufacturing and sale of the substance remain illegal. In contrast, legalization would abolish laws banning the possession and personal use of marijuana. There are costs and benefits associated with each approach, but the legalization of marijuana seems to be more helpful to society.

---

[215] ACLU, *Marijuana Arrests and Punishments* (April 5, 2022), https://www.aclu.org/other/marijuana-arrests-punishments

Proponents of decriminalizing marijuana argue that this approach sends the public conflicting messages because it gives the federal government authority to legalize marijuana while also regulating the use of the drug. Others claim that full legalization is too drastic and that it would confuse young Americans who are told to stay away from all types of drugs. It may entice the younger population to use the drug if there are no penalties for use of the substance. Although marijuana has not been reported to cause overdoses, it is still considered a "gateway drug" by many and it is not a substance Americans have completely accepted. There is a stigma against marijuana and advocates who favor legalization are hopeful that legalization will improve our crime rate and our economy.

Many states are decriminalizing marijuana as the country has softened its attitudes toward the drug. Decriminalization means the courts would impose fines rather than jail time on those arrested for possession of marijuana. This has allowed people to avoid having to struggle with the life-altering collateral consequences a criminal record carries, but fines can lead to large accruals of debt which is also damaging to their livelihoods, especially if these people are from economically disadvantaged backgrounds. A position where marijuana offenses carry larger consequences than other drugs like alcohol may be ineffective in such situations since cannabis does not seem to have the same detrimental impact on public health as alcohol or other substances of abuse.

Through the Compassionate Use Act of 1996 California became the first state to legalize marijuana for medicinal use by people with severe or chronic illnesses.[216] Since then, many states like Arizona, New Mexico, and South Dakota have followed California's example and legalized marijuana.[217] Marijuana has been shown to help many people who suffer from health complications, reducing pain from chronic diseases such as epilepsy and cancer.[218] The drug is said to alter pain pathways in the brain and make symptoms of illnesses more bearable. People who suffer from debilitating diseases like cancer should be able to use marijuana to relieve their pain without fear of being criminally prosecuted. Using the drug to help relieve pain and symptoms of chronic diseases may also contribute to a change in public opinion.

An article by Robert Schwartz in the *Canadian Medical Association Journal* explains that prohibition has barely reduced marijuana smoking and that the criminalization of the drug has had devastating consequences.[219] Prohibition has resulted in a disproportionate number of arrests and convictions of people caught with very small amounts of marijuana, leading to negative stereotypes surrounding minorities who are the main targets for arrest due to poor socioeconomic means to prevent their own incarceration. Black people and people of color are perceived to be associated with drugs more often than white people causing them to be arrested and convicted

---

[216] Compassionate Use Act of 1996, (11362.5 H&S)

[217] Business Insider, *States Where Marijuana,* https://www.businessinsider.com/legal-marijuana-states-2018-1, (last visited April 1, 2022).

[218] FDA, *Statement by FDA Commissioner Scott Gottlieb,* https://www.fda.gov/news-events/press-announcements/statement-fda-commissioner-scott-gottlieb-md-importance-conducting-proper-rese arch-prove-safe-and, (last visited April 5, 2022).

[219] Robert Schwartz, Legalize Marijuana Without the Smoke,189, Canadian Medical Association Journal (2017)

more frequently than white people. Schwartz proposes that along with the legalization of the drug, the country should expand public education, health warning labels, and more to ensure public safety. By educating citizens on drug use as a public health issue rather than a criminal issue, harmful stereotypes against POC may be reduced and public safety would increase.

As of now, there are 27 states that have decriminalized marijuana.[220] There are 18 states along with the District of Columbia that have legalized the drug.[221] Those who support legalization say that allowing the manufacturing and sale of the substance prohibits the industry from being concentrated in the black market. The regulation of marijuana sales makes it safer for consumers because there is more control over what chemicals and substances are allowed in the drug. It would provide a steady stream of new revenue for many states and the number of jobs would increase because the sale of the product would open people up to more career opportunities. The economy would benefit and public safety would also be improved. Regulation of marijuana would improve public health because people would be less likely to buy or use marijuana that has been tampered with.

[220] National Conference of State Legislatures, *Cannabis Overview*, https://www.ncsl.org/research/civil-and-criminal-justice/marijuana-overview.aspx#:~:text=Twenty%2Dseven%20states%20and%20the,no%20possibility%20of%20jail%20time), (last visited April 1, 2022).
[221] Business Insider, *States Where Marijuana*, https://www.businessinsider.com/legal-marijuana-states-2018-1, (last visited April 1, 2022).

CONCLUSION

The criminalization of many drugs, especially marijuana, in America has led to remarkably negative consequences including extreme racial disparities in arrests, convictions, and sentencing. Currently, a high number of people are incarcerated for possession of small amounts of cannabis even though the criminalization of this drug is societally unpopular. The legalization of marijuana will lessen the disproportionate number of arrests of Black people and POC for marijuana-related offenses and reduce negative collateral consequences to public health and public welfare. This approach will also afford terminally ill patients and people who struggle with painful illnesses a legal means of relieving their pain through using medical marijuana. The legal manufacturing and sale of this substance would create more job opportunities for Americans, thus restructuring the position of marijuana in the American economy. If the U.S. can reframe its approach to battling drug abuse through decriminalization, legalization, or by some other non-punitive strategy, then society will begin to see that the criminalization of cannabis is less effective than treating addiction as a public health problem. Reframing the U.S. approach should also center on drug abuse as a public health issue rather than a criminal issue.

UNITED STATES v. SAFEHOUSE: A SMALL CASE WITH BIG IMPLICATIONS

BY BEN PARSONS

INTRODUCTION

In 2020, the U.S. Attorney for the Eastern District of Pennsylvania filed a suit in the Third Circuit Court against Safehouse, a nonprofit in Philadelphia with plans to open the nation's first safe injection site. The safe injection site, a public health clinic with a harm reduction focus implemented in several European countries and Canada, provides a supervised location to oversee those injecting illicit drugs to provide information on addiction treatment and administer Naloxone to those who experience a drug overdose. The court found that such a location is illegal under the supremacy clause of the Constitution and the Controlled Substances Act.[222] In doing so, the district court not only limited the ability of states to change drug policy but also called into question the legality of the entire cannabis industry in the United States.

---

[222] US v. Safehouse, No. 20-1422 (2021).

ILLICIT DRUGS AND THE
CONTROLLED SUBSTANCES ACT:
A QUICK HISTORY

Though today America's strict enforcement of drug policies is well known, pre-1971 and Nixon's "War on Drugs", enforcement of drug policies were much more relaxed. In 1937, Congress passed the Marijuana Tax Act, creating an excise tax on cannabis growth, sales, and distribution regulating marijuana and other cannabis products through the Commerce Clause.[223] Eventually, this was overturned by the Supreme Court in the 1969 case *Leary v. US* (which found the Marijuana Tax Act was an unconstitutional form of self-incrimination)[224] and was replaced with the Controlled Substances Act of 1971.

The Controlled Substances Act of 1971 made multiple changes to US drug policy, with the most pertinent to today being the scheduling of drugs and the "crack house statute."[225] The schedules, known as Schedule I through V, sorted drugs into different categories of legality depending on their impacts with Schedule I being the most heavily regulated and Schedule V being the least.[226]

---

[223] *Did You Know... Marijuana Was Once a Legal Cross-Border Import*, US Customs and Border Patrol (Dec. 20 2019), https://www.cbp.gov/about/history/did-you-know/marijuana#:~:text=His%20campaign%20against%20Cannabis%20led,an%20annual%20tax%20of%2424 0%2424

[224] Leary v. US, 395 U.S. 6 (1969).

[225] *The Controlled Substances Act (CSA): A Legal Overview for the 117th Congress*, Congressional Research Service (Feb. 5 2021), https://sgp.fas.org/crs/misc/R45948.pdf

[226] Ibid.

Schedule I, for example, consists of drugs that "have no currently accepted medical use in the United States, a lack of accepted safety for use under medical supervision, and a high potential for abuse."[227] Schedule V, alternatively, consists of drugs that "have a low potential for abuse...and consist primarily of preparations containing limited quantities of certain narcotics."[228]

The other relevant aspect, as mentioned previously, is what is colloquially known as the "crack house statute." Know technically as 21 USC § 856, the crack house statute strengthens the power of the federal government to enforce the other regulations of the Controlled Substances Act by making it illegal to "knowingly open, lease, rent, use, or maintain any place, whether permanently or temporarily, for the purpose of manufacturing, distributing, or using any controlled substance."[229] In short, not only is using, possessing, and selling these drugs illegal, but it is also illegal to maintain a building of any sort that manufactures, distributes, or relates to illicit drugs in any way.

THE EVOLUTION OF THE WAR ON DRUGS: ADMITTING DEFEAT AND CHANGING POLICY

While a cursory reading of the Controlled Substances Act might not raise any hesitancy, when looking at the applications of the legislation today, views tend to change. One hesitancy, for example, is the fact that

---

[227] *Controlled Substance Schedules,* US Department of Justice, https://www.deadiversion.usdoj.g
ov/schedules/.
[228] Ibid.
[229] Controlled Substances Act, 21 USC § 856.

marijuana is considered a Schedule I drug.[230] Knowing
that marijuana has tangible medical benefits and that it
can, in fact, be used safely under medical supervision,
the idea that marijuana should be treated the same as
heroin and fentanyl is absurd.

Yet, what might be more concerning about the
Controlled Substances Act is the new understanding of
the law developed by *US v. Safehouse*. While the Eastern
District Court of Pennsylvania found that, since
Safehouse's goal was to ultimately reduce drug use, not
encourage it, the crack house statute did not apply, the
Third Circuit reversed this decision, saying that, despite
Safehouse's "benevolent motive" it "makes no
difference."[231] "Safehouse knows and intends that its
visitors will come with a significant purpose of doing
drugs, [thus] its safe-injection site will break the law."[232]

The court's argument is indisputable. Under the
Commerce Clause, Congress has the sole power of
"regulat[ing] Commerce with foreign Nations, and
among the several States, and with the Indian Tribes."[233]
Further, under the Supremacy Clause, it clearly states
that "This Constitution, and the Laws of the United
States…shall be the supreme Law of the Land; and the
Judges in every State shall be bound thereby, any Thing
in the Constitution or Laws of any State to the Contrary
notwithstanding."[234] There can be no question about it,

---

[230] *Controlled Substance Schedules,* US Department of Justice,
https://www.deadiversion.usdoj.g
ov/schedules/.
[231] US v. Safehouse, No. 20-1422 (2021).
[232] Ibid.
[233] U.S. Const. art I, § 8, cl. 3.
[234] U.S. Const. art VI, cl. 2.

not only is the crack house statute legal, but it also
overrides the power of state and local law.

The issue that comes with the court's argument is that it
calls into question the legality of one of the
fastest-growing sectors in the US economy: cannabis.
Federal law still classifies marijuana as a Schedule I
drug, making it illegal to possess, consume, buy, or
sell.[235] Yet, 37 states have legalized marijuana for
medical purposes and 18 have for recreational
purposes.[236] Does this mean that each of the 7,000 plus[237]
marijuana dispensaries across the United States illegal?
In theory, yes.

THE ETERNAL QUESTION OF FEDERALISM: SOLVING THE MARIJUANA POLICY GAP

Under both the Controlled Substances Act and this
ruling of US v. Safehouse, if the federal government
wanted to, it could arrest every single person - about
48.2 million people in the last year alone, who have

---

[235] *Controlled Substance Schedules,* US Department of Justice,
https://www.deadiversion.usdoj.g
ov/schedules/.

[236] Dan Avery, *Where Is Marijuana Legal? State Laws and
Federal Cannabis Legislation,* CNET (Apr. 11 2022),
https://www.cnet.com/news/politics/where-is-marijuana-legal-
state-laws-and-federal-cannabis-legi
slation/#:~:text=As%20of%20April%202022%2C%2037,New
%20Hampshire%2C%20New%20Jersey%2C%20New.

[237] Kait Hobson, *Study: 2020 Cannabis Dispensaries Growth,*
Mary Journal (Jan. 13 2020), https://ww
w.mary-magazine.com/health-wellness/study-2020-cannabis-d
ispensaries-growth/#:~:text=Now%2C%20as%20more%20sta
tes%20continue,7%2C490%20across%20the%20United%20S
tates.

consumed marijuana either medically or recreationally.[238] Fortunately, it seems that the government has no intention of doing this, but the mere fact that this could occur suggests policy change is needed. This could come in one of two forms - the federal government could simply refuse to prosecute places like Safehouse and marijuana dispensaries, allowing them to operate, or could amend the Controlled Substances Act narrowly, allowing both marijuana dispensaries and safe injection sites to operate in compliance with federal law. Immediate changes must be made to the United States' approach to drug policy in light of *US v. Safehouse*.

---

[238] *Marijuana and Public Health: Data and Statistics*, Center for Disease Control and Prevention (Jun. 8 2021), https://www.cdc.gov/marijuana/data-statistics.htm#:~:text=Ma rijuana%20is%20the%20most%20c ommonly,at%20least%20once%20in%202019.&text=Recent %20research%20estimated%20that%20approximately,marijua na%20have%20marijuana%20use%20disorder.

JUVENILE LIFE WITHOUT PAROLE AS CRUEL AND UNUSUAL PUNISHMENT

BY LAUREN GREENBERG

INTRODUCTION

Life without parole (LWOP) is typically seen as a more humane alternative to the death penalty. This may be true in the uniqueness and irrevocability of capital punishment, but many advocates and lifers themselves see life without parole as an extended death penalty. In her book, *A Woman Doing Life: Notes From A Prison for Women*, Erin George contends "we should be offered the opportunity to choose to be executed humanely instead of suffering a sad decline behind bars."[239] Life sentences are a more prolonged and painful punishment, as George describes. Not only are individuals sentenced to life without parole forced to watch their relationships degrade with limited contact, but they are subjected to

---

[239] George, Erin, Robert Johnson, and Alison Brooks Martin. A Woman Doing Life: Notes from a Prison for Women. Oxford University Press, 2015.

lousy food, subpar medical care, unsanitary living conditions, routine invasions of personal space and body, and abuse. Despite these conditions, America remains the only country "that sentences people to life without parole for crimes committed before turning 18."[240]

Advocates have argued for abolition of juvenile life without parole sentences because they perpetuate racial disparities through sentencing discretion. Since Black children are often viewed as older than their white peers they are subject to more harsh penalties under the law. Twenty-five states and the District of Columbia have banned juvenile life without parole (JLWOP), that is for those under 18. In nine other states, no one currently serves LWOP if they committed their offense under 18. In total 34 states in some way denounce the punishment either through legislation or judicial discretion in sentencing.

Despite advancements toward abolition, 17 states still allow children to be sentenced indefinitely with no chance of getting out, supporting the belief that children are incapable of rehabilitation, or as the Court has routinely said, that they are "permanently incorrigible." In five core Supreme Court cases surrounding this topic– *Roper v. Simmons* (2005), *Graham v. Florida* (2010), *Miller v. Alabama* (2012), *Montgomery v. Louisiana* (2016), and *Jones v. Mississippi* (2021)– the Justices established and upheld that "children are constitutionally different from adults in their levels of culpability."[241]

---

[240] Rovner, Josh. "Juvenile Life without Parole: An Overview." The Sentencing Project, June 7, 2021. https://www.sentencingproject.org/publications/juvenile-life-without-parole/.

[241] Rovner. "Juvenile Life without Parole: An Overview."

These differences in accountability and maturity inform how judges interpret the Eighth Amendment's protection from cruel and unusual punishment during sentencing, but they only limit, not eradicate, the possibility of a child dying in prison. Drawing from the Court's reasoning in *Roper v. Simmons* that children are too constitutionally different from adults to be sentenced to the death penalty, the punishment of life without parole is also disproportionate to their youthful status.[242] A ban on this cruel and unusual form of punishment for a child should be explored by all states, if not federally, if we wish to stray from unnecessarily punitive measures that denounce rehabilitation and perpetuate racial disparities.

HISTORY: JUVENILE SENTENCING AND PERMANENT INCORRIGIBILITY

From the early 2000's onwards, the Court has evolved in its thinking surrounding juvenile sentencing. In the 2005 case *Roper v. Simmons*, the Court struck down the death penalty for people under 18, reasoning that the punishment is "so disproportionate as to be 'cruel and unusual,'" and its abolition for juveniles is required by the Eighth Amendment.[243] The majority also cited diminished culpability, "lack of control over their immediate surroundings" which should forgive them "for failing to escape negative influences," and "susceptibility to immature and irresponsible behavior [that] means... their irresponsible conduct is not as morally reprehensible as that of an adult."[244] The Court in *Roper* also supported its opinion by stating that "a

---

[242] Roper v. Simmons, 543 U.S. 551 (2005)
[243] Roper v. Simmons (2005)
[244] Ibid

national consensus [that] has developed against the execution of juvenile offenders... [and] the imposition of the juvenile death penalty has become truly unusual over the last decade."[245] Although the imposition of juvenile life without parole is not yet unusual, 34 states have in some way rebuked its use.

The 2010 case *Graham v. Florida* invalidated life without parole sentences for people under 18 convicted of non-homicide crimes. Justice Kennedy, writing the majority opinion, argued that punishment for the crime must be proportional to the offense, and since the culpability of children can be distinguished from that of adults, the Eighth Amendment was violated.[246] Again the Court noted a national consensus against JLWOP considering its sparse implementation.

In 2012, *Miller v. Alabama* recognized the great need to protect almost all children from LWOP notwithstanding the crime. It established that a mandatory sentence of juvenile life without parole is unconstitutional, relying on the principle in *Roper* and *Graham* "that judges need to consider the qualities of youthful defendants to deal out 'a fair and individualized sentence.'"[247] Justice Elena Kagan added that adolescence is defined by "transient rashness, proclivity for risk, and inability to assess consequences... [which lessens] a child's 'moral culpability'" and makes it more likely that, as development occurs, deficits will be rectified.[248] The Court's reasoning lends itself to the idea that punishment dealt to juvenile offenders should be less than that of

---

[245] Ibid
[246] Graham v. Florida, 560 U.S. 48 (2010)
[247] Miller v. Alabama, 567 U.S. 460 (2012)
[248] Ibid

their adult counterparts. The fourth case, *Montgomery v. Louisiana*, was a simple clarification that *Miller* applied retroactively.[249] In other words, all children previously subject to a mandatory LWOP sentence would have their cases reevaluated by parole boards.

The most recent case, *Jones v. Mississippi* (2021), stepped away from the holdings in previous cases, contending that a recorded factual finding of "permanent incorrigibility" during sentencing is not required to impose a sentence of JLWOP.[250] Justice Sotomayor dissented, arguing that the Court circumvented its precedent by interpreting *Miller* to mean a judge can use discretion in taking youth into account rather than having to follow standard sentencing practice. Rather, *Miller* required that "a sentencer... 'make th[e] judgment' that the juvenile in question is one of those rare children for whom LWOP is a constitutionally permissible sentence."[251] This *Miller* requirement that solely incorrigible children be sentenced to LWOP raises the question of why it is lawfully permitted under *Jones* for a judge to "impose such a sentence without actually deciding if the juvenile before the court is permanently incorrigible."[252] Prior to this case, the Court required a finding of incorrigibility because children are unique in their characteristics and are, of anyone, the most capable

---

[249] Montgomery v. Louisiana, 577 U.S. __ (2016)
[250] Jones v. Mississippi, 593 U.S. __ (2021)
[251] Miller v. Alabama, 567 U.S. 460 (2012)
[252] Shapiro, David M., and Monet Gonnerman. "To the States: Reflections on Jones v. Mississippi." Harvard Law Review, November 20, 2021.
https://harvardlawreview.org/2021/11/to-the-states-reflections-on-jones-v-mississippi/.

of reform as they develop. Instead, the majority in *Jones* disregards this obligation.

STATES AGREE, JUVENILE LIFE WITHOUT PAROLE IS CRUEL AND UNUSUAL

In a 2016 decision, *State v. Sweet,* the Iowa Supreme Court found that all juvenile life without parole sentences violate the state constitution's ban on cruel and unusual punishment. The court cited U.S. Supreme Court decisions that focused on proportionality of offenses, noting the consideration of this Eighth Amendment tenet as a requirement for justice under the law.[253] The Iowa court also relied on key reasonings in *Furman v. Georgia* (1972) and *Gregg v. Georgia* (1976), arguing that "the Supreme Court... was clearly concerned about the arbitrary nature of the imposition of the death penalty and the need to focus its application on only the most deserving offenders."[254] This is generalizable to juvenile life without parole because children should not be considered deserving offenders based on the Court's rationale in *Roper, Graham,* and *Miller* that juveniles have diminished levels of culpability in their crimes. The Court concluded that "because the signature qualities of youth are transient, incorrigibility is inconsistent with youth," meaning that no child should be sentenced to life in prison without the possibility of parole review.

The Massachusetts court's decision, *Diatchenko v. Dist. Attorney*, in 2013 similarly held that a sentence of JLWOP violates the state's Eighth Amendment "because it is an unconstitutionally disproportionate punishment

---

[253] State v. Sweet, 879 N.W.2d 811 (Iowa 2016)
[254] Ibid

when viewed in the context of the unique characteristics of juvenile offenders."[255] Both the Iowa and Massachusetts supreme courts rely on the reasoning of the highest court in the land to justify their decisions that JLWOP is far from consistent with how the term youth has legally and socially been defined. Their arguments lend themselves to the reasoning that juvenile life without parole should no longer exist.

JUVENILES AS A UNIQUE
CLASS OF DEFENDANTS

A minor is not capable of the same critical thinking skills as an adult. Thus, holding them to the same standards during sentencing is unjust. The American Psychological Association's Amicus Brief in *Roper v. Simmons* makes this distinction clear, noting that adolescents, as a group, "are not yet mature in ways that affect their decision-making."[256] Behavioral studies prove that they are "less likely to consider alternative courses of action, understand the perspective of others, and restrain impulses."[257] During this period of life the brain has not yet reached maturity, specifically the frontal lobe, which controls decision making. The *Graham* decision highlighted this necessity of giving children a chance at rehabilitation because scientific distinctions between juveniles and adults are so compelling.

---

[255] Diatchenko v. Dist. Attorney, 466 Mass. 655 (Mass. 2013)
[256] "Roper v. Simmons." American Psychological Association. American Psychological Association.
https://www.apa.org/about/offices/ogc/amicus/roper.
[257] Ibid

For individuals under 18, there is legal precedent in drawing lines here. We restrict children younger than 18 from serving in the military, consuming alcohol, serving on juries, or viewing certain movies because state governments have intelligently decided that individuals under 18 are not mature or culpable enough. From both the highest U.S. Court and state statutes, America has drawn these lines. Yet, it holds children to the same standards in terms of harsh sentencing to life without parole. The Court, prior to *Jones v. Mississippi*, made clear that children are constitutionally different. The Court decisions and state categorizations of children lend themselves to an argument that life without parole sentences should not be permissible. They disregard the distinct characteristics of juveniles, ensuring that there is no proportionality in sentencing.

INTERVENING RATIONALES

Abolition of juvenile life without parole is essential because the punishment entrenches injustices already faced by children. In fact, those sentenced to JLWOP tend to be victims themselves. In a 2012 survey by the Sentencing Project of juveniles sentenced to life without parole, "79% witnessed violence in their homes regularly, 32% grew up in public housing, fewer than half were attending school at the time of their offense, 47% were physically abused, 80% of girls reported histories of physical abuse, and 77% of girls reported histories of sexual abuse."[258] While state and federal governments spend money attempting to incarcerate children who have largely been failed, these funds would be better spent attempting to support children before they are brought to the legal system at all. Even more

---

[258] Rovner. "Juvenile Life without Parole: An Overview."

concerning about the harsh punishment of LWOP is that not all children are equally subjected to the sentence. Of those individuals currently serving JLWOP, 62% percent are Black. White children with Black victims are only half as likely (3.6%) to receive a sentence of life without parole as are Black children with white victims. Although, theoretically, sentencing should be based on actual age and perceived culpability Black children are routinely perceived as older, subjecting them to life without parole sentences more often than their white peers. They disparately receive more cruel punishments under the law because they are seen as less youthful and thus more culpable in the eyes of decision makers.

RECOMMENDATIONS

Supreme Court precedent and 34 states rebuking the use of JLWOP provides evidence that the nation is shifting away from this harsh punishment. Since the country is increasingly recognizing the diminished culpability of juveniles as a class, JLWOP sentences should be declared unconstitutional nationwide. If proclaimed goals of rehabilitation are to be fulfilled there must be a meaningful opportunity for release. After *Jones*, there is little reason to believe that the Supreme Court will rule juvenile life without parole unconstitutional. But many state supreme courts have already been inclined to go beyond what the Constitution requires. In the absence of federal action, state supreme courts can interpret their Constitutions to guarantee more rights to safeguard against cruel and unusual punishment since the United States Constitution is a floor, not a ceiling. This is very practicable, and some state constitutions, like Washington, currently provide more protection than the Eighth Amendment itself.

Even though the Supreme Court has differently decided guidelines for children under 18, the lines are still blurry between childhood and adulthood. The Washington Supreme Court echoed this sentiment, interpreting its Eighth Amendment protection to a greater extent than the U.S. Constitution, and barring mandatory LWOP sentences for young adults, not only juveniles. This is exemplified in *In re Pers. Restraint of Monschke* where the court was asked whether a sentencing authority "must exercise discretion when sentencing any 18, 19, or 20 year old to life in prison without parole".[259] They argued that defendants "were essentially juveniles in all but name at the time of their crimes" so life without parole was "unconstitutionally cruel" and their sentences were reversed.[260] They maintained that "modern social science, our precedent, and a long history of arbitrary line drawing have all shown that no clear line exists between childhood and adulthood."[261] It is murky as to what age someone is fully developed in their culpability, and many studies show adult brains are not developed until the age of twenty-five or later for some individuals.[262] The Washington court follows this scientifically backed research in its reasoning. States can and should provide greater protection from sentences of juvenile life without parole to young people who are essentially children at the time of their crimes.

---

[259] In re Pers. Restraint of Monschke, 482 P.3d 276 (Wash. 2021)

[260] Ibid

[261] Ibid

[262] Blakemore, Sarah-Jayne. "The Mysterious Workings of the Adolescent Brain." Sarah-Jayne Blakemore: The mysterious workings of the adolescent brain | TED Talk, June 2012. https://www.ted.com/talks/sarah_jayne_blakemore_the_myste rious_workings_of_the_adolescent_brain?language=en.

CONCLUSION

Largely, the United States' great reliance on Life Without Parole says that someone cannot be saved, that they are unredeemable. If this is least true for anyone, it is juveniles who have worse decision-making skills, lessened culpability, greater impulsivity, and have not yet developed as people. Sentences that terminate the potential for second chances and rehabilitation are inhumane and inappropriate, especially for children. Considering the Court's decision in *Roper v. Simmons* that children are too unique in their status to be sentenced to death, life without parole is not commensurate with their status either.[263] Since the Court has already rebuked capital punishment for juveniles, it should follow that life without parole is abolished since between both punishments the only possibility for release is death. With a sentence of life without parole children will spend their entire livelihood subject to the isolation and violence of prison and, similar to spending years on death row, will never again see the outside world.

Abolition of juvenile life without parole is essential if the United States wishes to nurture children. Instead of subjecting individuals with diminished culpability to harsh punishments, government funds would be better spent positively supporting children in their youth—fostering better schools that stray from the school to prison pipeline, and addressing factors like poverty, abuse, and high dropout rates that are too often indicators of future involvement in the justice system. This cruel and unusual punishment should be wholly banned for children if the United States wishes to move

---

[263] Roper v. Simmons, 543 U.S. 551 (2005)

past needlessly punitive measures that sustain racial disparities and rebuke rehabilitation.

The American University
Undergraduate Law Journal

AU UNDERGRAD
LAW JOURNAL

EDUCATION LAW

COLUMN

THE CASE FOR AFFIRMATIVE ACTION

BY NOAH GOCIAL

INTRODUCTION

Affirmative Action is at the forefront of the intersection between education and civil rights. It comes after much legal precedent that struck down separate but equal, upheld laws that protected groups previously discriminated against, and explores the prejudice and guardrails that still limit freedom for all. Using said precedent, and exploring the plethora of legal frameworks and opinions, this paper will argue that Affirmative Action is not only Constitutionally sound, but encouraged

BACKGROUND

Earning his title of "The Great Dissenter" by creating legal frameworks that would eventually become supreme law out of disagreeing with the majority opinion, Justice John Marshall Harlan paved the way for early racial

THE AMERICAN UNIVERSITY
UNDERGRADUATE LAW JOURNAL

equality. His dissent in *Plessy v. Ferguson* (1896) stated "Our constitution is colorblind... in respect of civil rights, all citizens are equal before the law... It [segregation] cannot be justified upon any legal grounds," in response to Justice Henry Billings Browns' insistence that segregation is needed and beneficial. The dissenter found himself at odds with the nigh unanimous verdict, and wrote this law in accordance with his belief that racism had no place in the founding documents. The author, Peter Canellos, furthers this sentiment in the *Insular Cases*[264] (1901) where he writes, in another dissenting opinion, "the idea that this country may acquire territories anywhere upon the earth... and hold them as mere colonies or provinces... [and they] enjoy only such rights as Congress chooses to accord them, is wholly inconsistent with the spirit and... the words, of the Constitution." Harlan, in this dissent, went beyond recognition of the issue; he encouraged the idea that, in order to attain equal rights, changes had to be made to the very foundation of colonization. In the former, Harlan made it clear that every citizen is equal before the law, in the latter, he expanded on this and stated that every citizen has the rights of the full constitution, and should, furthermore, be allowed to capitalize on it however they can. In both of these cases, he laid the framework that would be applied in contemporary Civil Rights cases, including Affirmative Action, that defined

---

[264] The case defining whether or not the United States extends full Constitutional rights to the colonies and citizens of Puerto Rico and Hawaii as a side to whether or not these colonies apply as 'foreign countries' in relation to tariffs.

how the government could act when defending equal rights and extending those rights to the individual.[265]

RECTIFYING PAST ILLS:

Civil Rights have always been a contentious issue. Regardless of the time period, it has stretched between deference to states or to precedent. In *City of Richmond v. J.A. Croson Company* (1988), the court found that a law, passed in Richmond, which required construction companies to subcontract at least 30 percent of their business to minority contractors, lacked approval from the Equal Protections clause of the 14th Amendment. In her majority opinion, Justice O'Connor wrote "the stated interest of providing a remedy for past discrimination in the construction industry is not compelling, based on evidence that shows little previous discrimination in this area." Plainly, O'Connor gave her, and the courts, approval to have such a quota if it proved to be a remedy for past discrimination. The qouta for past discrimination is a legal framework not entirely explored in contemporary America. Yet, it can prove, since Slavery, Black Codes, Jim Crow Laws and segregation, that Black Americans have been descriminated – specifically in the education system – and therefore can meet this quota. Thurgood Marshall, in a dissenting opinion to that case, stated that "the record does show that the construction industry had been subject to discriminatory practices." The disagrement came down to if justices felt there was a history of discrimination, not the legality of

---

[265] Canellos, Peter S. *The Great Dissenter: The Story of John Marshall Harlan, America's Judicial Hero.* Simon & Schuster, 2021. P 360.

such an act, which gives credence to Affirmative Action.[266]

CONTEMPORARY FIXES:

In *Fisher v. University of Texas* (2013), a student had been denied entry into the school and filed suit because she felt the University's use of race as a deciding factor violated the Equal Protections Clause. The court decided that strict scrutiny, or what is in the best interest of the government, had to be applied; and the overall expansion of diversity did meet the requirement it set, and therefore race could be a defining factor.[267]

The *City of Richmond* case set the precedent that there needed to be a compelling inequity in order for the government to act, which it is when looking into the secondary education system and admissions. *Fisher* set the precedent that race-based admissions is not a violation of the 15th Amendment, solidifying the government's capacity in intervening in such a matter. As there is a history of universities denying students based on them being black,[268] Justice O'Connor concurres: Affirmative Action aims to rectify that past injury.

---

[266] City of Richmond v. J. A. Croson Co., 488 U.S. 469 (1989). (14th Amendment and the implications for justifying past descrimination)

[267] Fisher v. University of Texas. 579 U.S. 365 (more)136 S. Ct. 2198; 195 L. Ed. 2d 511. 2012. (14th Amendment and the factor of race-based admissions)

[268] Harris, Leslie M. "The Forgotten Racist Past of American Universities." *The New Republic.* https://newrepublic.com/article/121382/forgotten-racist-past-american-universities. March 2015.

FLORIDA "DON'T SAY GAY BILL"

BY ALEXIS SALDANA

BACKGROUND:

The Florida House Committee recently passed a bill that bans the discussion of sexual orientation and gender in classrooms. The Republican majority in the House of Education and Employment Committee passed the Parental Rights in Education bill or HB 1557 which has since earned the name of the "Don't Say Gay Bill" due to the ban on significant speech surrounding sexual orientation.[269] The bill states that schools should create an environment in which the responsibility of making decisions regarding the upbringing of children should be left to parents rather than schools.[270] There is also a requirement stipulated in the bill for updated procedures for school districts, administrators, and teachers as well as updated materials that avoid discussions on gender or sexual orientation.[271] It also specifies that any person

---

[269] House Bill 1557: Parental Rights Education, Education and Employment Committee, Florida
[270] *Id.*
[271] *Id.*

within the school district must provide notification to parents when schools discuss critical decisions involving the mental, emotional, or physical well-being of students.[272] The bill states that any discussion of these matters is prohibited in primary grade levels, and if any parent feels that a teacher or administrator violates this bill then the parent has a right to sue the district for violating their right to teach their own children on these sensitive matters. As a result of the passing of this act, school administrations will update standards and educator practices to fit the guidelines of this bill.[273]

CURRENT LEGISLATION AND RECENT PRECEDENT:

Just recently in 2021, President Biden released an executive order in which he laid out specific terms that the United States government will abide by regarding transgender rights and discrimination based on sexual orientation and gender identity.[274] After the executive order was put into motion, the Department of Education released a fact sheet that specifically stipulated the anti-discrimination parameters of the executive order including offering gender-neutral bathrooms in public

---

[272] *Id.*

[273] Alfonseca, Kierra. *abc News.* "Don't Say Gay bill moves forward in Florida." 26 January 2022. https://abcnews.go.com/US/dont-gay-bill-moves-forward-flori da/story?id=82481565

[274] Executive Order 13988-Preventing and Combating Discrimination on the Basis of Gender Identity or Sexual Orientation". Government. Office of the Federal Register, National Archives and Records Administration, January 19, 2021

high schools.[275] The Department of Education is currently being sued for this fact sheet due to its inconsistencies with the rulings of the case that the executive order was developed from, *Boystock v. Clayton County* (2020).[276] This case specified protections for transgender employees in the workplace, which were then extended to schools through the executive order administered by President Biden, and the fact sheet produced by the Department of Education.[277][278] Though the fact sheet is under review in the lawsuit, the executive order still remains and therefore provides a precedent for transgender rights and anti-discrimination orders for public high schools.

Title IX also provides protections against discrimination in the workplace and at school.[279] The protections in the law cover the basis of sex, sexual identity, age, race, and

---

[275] Education Amendments Act of 1972, 20 U.S.C. §§1681 - 1688 (2018) (Title IX) "DCPD-202100057

[276] *Bostock v. Clayton County, Georgia.* (United States Court of Appeals 11th Circuit Dec. June 15, 2020). *Plaintiffs v. United States Department of Education.* United States District Court for the Eastern District of Tennessee Knoxville Division. Case No. 3: 21-cv-00308

[277] Executive Order 13988-Preventing and Combating Discrimination on the Basis of Gender Identity or Sexual Orientation". Government. Office of the Federal Register, National Archives and Records Administration, January 19, 2021

[278] "Supporting Intersex Students" Department of Education. *Office for Civil Rights* (October 2021). https://www2.ed.gov/about/offices/list/ocr/docs/ocr-factsheet-intersex-202110.pdf

[279] Education Amendments Act of 1972, 20 U.S.C. §§1681 - 1688 (2018) (Title IX) "DCPD-202100057

more. The law is specifically tailored to prevent discrimination against anything that harms a person's identity in the workplace, on school campuses, in athletics, etc.[280] This law contains an incredible breadth of protections for specific identities, and it is the most important precedent for anti-discrimination cases because the law is so specific and because the variety of lawsuits that have been filed under Title IX is so varied. Between Title IX and recent legislation, there is significant precedent for transgender rights and anti-discrimination for sexual orientation and gender identity that could undermine the recent bill passed in Florida that would limit the discussion of these identities as a whole.

RAMIFICATIONS:

There are several states who are following the Florida bill with similar legislation with an estimation of about 15 total states to propose legislation within the next year.[281] Kansas is proposing a bill to increase transparency in schools so that there is a heightened awareness of the content of instruction in schools.[282] This bill in Kansas has a similar goal to the legislation passed in Florida as both bills are attempting to provide parents with the opportunity to teach their children about sexuality without the interference of schools.[283] The Kansas bill does have many other topics included in the legislation such as allowing parents to decide whether or

---

[280] *Id.* Title IX
[281] Dahl, Richard. *Find Law.* "Understanding Florida's 'Don't Say Gay' Bill" 10 March 2022.
https://www.findlaw.com/legalblogs/law-and-life/understanding-floridas-dont-say-gay-bill/
[282] Kansas House Bill 2662
[283] *Id* House Bill 2662

not to vaccinate their students, or which vaccinations to give their students.[284] There are also specifications within the bill that provide parameters in which schools have to specifically give more transparency to parents in all school material including lessons, surveys, syllabi, handouts, and examinations.[285] Indiana also has a similar bill being discussed that addresses inappropriate materials being taught to students including discussions of sexuality and sex.[286] The Indiana legislation has a stronger focus on the students rather than the parents in the language of the bill which differs from the Florida legislation which focuses more on the parents rather than the students.[287] While many of the newer bills being discussed in other states often have milder language than the Florida bill, as seen in the Indiana legislation, the effects will largely be the same. More states are expected to follow Florida with similar legislation in order to limit the conversations surrounding sexuality in schools. This is concerning for many gay rights advocates and citizens across the country as there are fears that these bills could silence many students in the classroom. There are several attempts at lawsuits against the Florida bill but none have reached the courts quite yet so the legal ramifications of this legislation are still unknown.

CONCLUSION:

The Florida legislation passed in the House Bill of 1557 will have significant impacts on schools and students everywhere. As more and more states follow in the footsteps of Florida's legislators and there are no

---

[284] *Id* House Bill 2662
[285] *Id* House Bill 2662
[286] Indiana House Bill 1040
[287] *Id* House Bill 1040

lawsuits to prevent this type of legislation, the rights of LGBTOIA+ students may be set back for decades. There will likely be many lawsuits based on the legislation in Florida and perhaps on other similar legislation such as Kansas or Indiana, but the fact that this bill was presented and passed into legislation is extremely jarring. Gay rights have been making great strides in recent decades but the new attitude of extreme partisanship within the U.S politics today has provided grounds for more extreme legislation. It is not yet clear how this bill will directly affect students and schools in Florida, however, by limiting the freedom to speak about issues regarding sexuality the results of this bill might turn out very negatively.

THE AMERICAN UNIVERSITY
UNDERGRADUATE LAW JOURNAL

AU UNDERGRAD
LAW JOURNAL

ENTERTAINMENT

LAW

COLUMN

A LEAGUE BUILT UPON BIAS

BY CAMERON CRAWFORD

INTRODUCTION

In February of 2022, Brian Flores, former head coach of the Miami Dolphins NFL team, filed a lawsuit against the NFL, accusing the league of discriminating against black coaches in its hiring process and unequal opportunities and pay, compared to white coaches.[288] Flores, one of the few black coaches in the NFL, claimed that he was invited to "sham" interviews, where he had no genuine shot at being accepted for a coaching position. His reasoning for this statement is that three days before his interview for the New York Giants head coaching position, Bill Belichek, the New England Patriots head coach and a top ranked coach in the league, messaged Flores, telling him that he had the position nearly secured already. Yet, Belichek meant to send the text to Brian Daboll, a white coach who ended up getting

---

[288] Mark Maske and Nicki Jhabvala, *Former Dolphins coach Brian Flores sues NFL and its teams, alleging racial discrimination,* (Feb. 1, 2022, 8:52 PM), https://www.washingtonpost.com/sports/2022/02/01/brian-flor es-lawsuit-nfl-discrimination/

the position. When Flores asked Belichek if he had meant to send the text to him, Belichek responded "Sorry--I [messed] this up. I double checked and misread the text. I think they are naming Brian Daboll. I'm sorry about that. BB."[289] All of this occurred before Flores' interview, which led him to believe that he had no chance at being offered the position and was just being interviewed so that the team met diversity requirements. Flores filed the lawsuit in the U.S. District Court for the Southern District of New York.

Furthermore, Flores was fired from the Miami Dolphins head coach position, despite having two winning seasons in a row. The Dolphins owner, Stephen Ross, instructed Flores to "tank," or intentionally lose games, in order to secure a high draft pick. Flores was appalled at this and was characterized by the media as someone who is difficult to work with and aggressive, a racist stereotype frequently given to people of color in high positions.

HISTORICAL BACKGROUND

The Civil Rights Act of 1964 was a landmark piece of legislation that "prohibits employment discrimination based on race, color, religion, sex and national origin," under Title VII of the Act.[290] However, the NFL is no stranger to accusations of racial bias. Many people are familiar with Colin Kaepernick and his "blackball" from the NFL. In the summer of 2016, there were a number of shootings of unarmed black men, so Kaepernick, who is also a black man, began to protest at games by kneeling during the National Anthem. Throughout the 2016

---

[289] Id.

[290] Title VII of the Civil Rights Act of 1964, 42 U.S.C. § 88-352.

season, some teammates began to join him in his protest
and there was huge outcry by the public. Yet, Kaepernick
did not want to support a flag representing a country that
perpetuated staunch mistreatment of black people.
Following the 2016 season, Kaepernick's contract ended
and he was not signed by any NFL teams, despite being
a promising young quarterback with great potential.[291]

The league has also previously been involved with a
practice called "race norming," wherein brain testing for
NFL concussion victims is race-based.[292] The NFL
agreed to stop race-norming practices last year, but
formerly, dementia testing was adjusted based on race,
making it extremely difficult for black retired players
who had suffered brain injuries to earn damages in
lawsuits. It was a racist practice built upon the idea that
black players have a lower cognitive base level than
those of other races. Aside from being completely
untrue, this is inherently discriminatory, as 70% of active
players are black, yet white players were receiving about
two or three times as much money than black
counterparts in settlements.[293] At the time of the NFL
policy change that reversed race-norming, 2,000 players

[291] Cindy Boren, *A timeline of Colin Kaepernick's protests
against police brutality, four years after they began,* (Aug. 26,
2020),
https://www.washingtonpost.com/sports/2020/06/01/colin-kae
pernick-kneeling-history/
[292] Matt Rourke, *NFL agrees to end race-based brain testing
in $1B settlement on concussions,* (Oct. 20, 2021, 10:14 PM),
https://www.npr.org/2021/10/20/1047793751/nfl-concussion-s
ettlement-race-norming-cte#:~:text=Tiny%20Desk%20Contes
t-,NFL%20agrees%20to%20end%20race%2Dbased%20brain
%20testing%20in%20%241,players%20to%20win%20dement
ia%20awards
[293] *Id.*

had applied for dementia rewards and only 30% were approved.[294]

The NFL has a bad track record regarding diversity and inclusion with their coaching staff and front office employees. As it currently stands, there are only two black head coaches of 32 NFL teams: Mike Tomlin of the Pittsburgh Steelers and Lovie Smith of the Houston Texans.[295] At the time of Flores' lawsuit, there have been a total of 141 white head coaches hired since 1989 (the first year a black coach was hired) and just 19 black coaches.[296] This is a stark discrepancy, given that 70% of NFL players are black. In an attempt to encourage diverse hiring practices, the league introduced the Rooney Rule in 2003. The Rooney Rule sought to give benefits to teams that interviewed and/or hired black coaches. The policy initially required each team to interview at least one racial minority when looking to hire a new head coach.[297] In 2009, the rule was expanded to apply to General Manager and other front office positions.[298] In 2020, the policy was amended so that teams were rewarded draft compensation for developing minority talent that became a head coach or General Manager.[299] Finally, in 2021, the rule changed so that

---

[294] Id.
[295] Kent Babb, Andrew Golden and Mark Maske, *The Brian Flores experience? 'That's the reality for most Black coaches.'*, (Feb. 6, 2022, 5:00 AM), https://www.washingtonpost.com/sports/2022/02/06/brian-flores-black-coaches-interviews/
[296] Id.
[297] The Rooney Rule, https://operations.nfl.com/inside-football-ops/diversity-inclusion/the-rooney-rule/
[298] Id.
[299] Id.

teams were required to interview at least two racial minorities for vacant head coaching positions and one for coordinator positions.[300] Yet, the Rooney Rule has received criticism, as diversity amongst coaching and front office positions has actually lowered and the rule has resulted in sham interviews, such as those of Brian Flores.[301]

IMPACT AND CONCLUSION

Recently, Flores was hired by the Pittsburgh Steelers as a senior defensive assistant and linebackers coach.[302] In Pittsburgh, he will be coaching alongside Mike Tomlin, one of two black NFL head coaches and arguably the league's best head coach. In his first interview as a new member of Pittsburgh's coaching staff, Flores explained that he refused to sign a non-disparagement agreement (NDA), so that he could speak out about his experiences.[303] An NDA ensures that one will not make any defamatory or disparaging remarks about a company or its people to any person or in any public forum.[304] Flores and his attorneys explained that by not signing the

---

[300] *Id.*

[301] Kent Babb, Andrew Golden and Mark Maske.

[302] Nicole Acevedo, *Pittsburgh Steelers hire Brian Flores after coach files racial discrimination suit against NFL*, (Feb. 19, 2022, 3:23 PM), https://www.nbcnews.com/news/sports/pittsburgh-steelers-hire-brian-flores-coach-files-racial-discriminatio-rcna16961

[303] Wayne Sterling, *Former Miami Dolphins head coach Brian Flores claims he was offered money to keep quiet after firing*, (Feb. 23, 2022, 9:43 AM), https://www.cnn.com/2022/02/23/sport/brian-flores-nfl-coach-dolphins/index.html

[304] Non-Disparagement Sample Clauses, Law Insider, https://www.lawinsider.com/clause/non-disparagement

agreement, he missed out on millions of dollars, in what would have been an incentive to silence Flores about his experience with the Dolphins and the owner's request for Flores to tank the team.

Flores is not alone in the discrimination he faces from the NFL as a black man. Eric Bieniemy, the offensive coordinator for the Kansas City Chiefs, is one of the NFL's most talented coaches, yet continues to be declined head coaching positions. The league's racial disparities can be clearly seen in the amount of white coaches versus black coaches, both historically and currently. Although Flores' lawsuit is still in the early stages, he has brought a great deal of pressure and attention onto the NFL, in an attempt to foster positive changes and a more equitable league.

THE LEGAL CONTEXT OF CROWD CRUSH IN THE WAKE OF ASTROWORLD

BY DIANA GERTSENSHTEYN

INTRODUCTION

On November 5th, 2021, American recording artist Travis Scott, in partnership with entertainment company Live Nation, held his annual music festival "Astroworld" in Houston, Texas. What ensued was a mass casualty event, costing the lives of ten people and injuring hundreds[305]. The tragedy occurred as a result of a phenomenon called crowd crush, in which the density of a crowd results in individuals either not being able to breathe or being trampled upon due to the sheer force of a surge[306]. Since the incident, over 300 lawsuits,

---

[305] Jon Blistein, *Astroworld Victims Died of 'Compression Asphyxia,' Medical Examiner Determines*, Music News (Dec. 16, 2021, 4:15 PM) https://www.rollingstone.com/music/music-news/astroworld-victims-cause-of-death-1272930/

[306] Stan Choe, *Explainer: Here is why crowd surges can kill people,* Arts & Culture (Nov. 9, 2021 1:53 PM)

collectively worth billions of dollars, were filed and subsequently merged into one case, heard by one judge, per the request of parties to litigation[307]. Scott, Live Nation, guest performer Drake, and other parties that collaborated on the event were all named. Additionally, the House Committee and Oversight and Reform announced a bipartisan probe into Live Nation's complicity in the tragedy on December 21st, 2021[308].

The suits were filed on the basis of a legal concept called premise liability law, in which an injured individual must prove that "anyone who is connected with the ownership of a venue used for public entertainment, and anyone who promotes, manages, or performs in a public entertainment venue" was negligent in respect to the property, resulting in injury or death[309]. This means that for the owner or organizer to be found responsible, they must have been aware that the area was unsafe and neglected to work towards a safer environment.

Amidst the continued outrage and legal battles, it is important to remember that this incident is merely the

---

https://www.pbs.org/newshour/arts/explainer-here-is-why-crowd-surges-can-kill-people

[307] Kimberlee Speakman, *Nearly 300 Astroworld Lawsuits To Be Combined Into Single Case*, Forbes (Dec. 3, 2021, 8:39pm) https://www.forbes.com/sites/kimberleespeakman/2021/12/03/nearly-300-astroworld-lawsuits-to-be-combined-into-single-case/?sh=73b63ee0294d

[308] *Maloney, Comer Lead Members in Launching Bipartisan Investigation into Live Nation's Role in Astroworld Tragedy,* House Committee on Oversight and Reform (Dec. 22, 2021) https://oversight.house.gov/news/press-releases/maloney-comer-lead-members-in-launching-bipartisan-investigation-into-live

[309] C. Barry Montgomery and Bradley C. Nahrstadt, *Virginia Sports and Entertainment Law Journal* 3 (2003-2004).

latest in a history of crowd crush casualties born out of negligence and poor planning. It is important to reflect on the history of such events to evaluate possible solutions going forward.

BACKGROUND

Beyond music-oriented events like concerts and large festivals, crowd crush has occurred at sporting events, major sales at department stores, and nightclubs[310]. Famous examples are mass casualties at Hillsborough stadium, a Long Island Walmart on Black Friday, and a The Who concert[311]. The common denominator is large, dense crowds, and poor planning. In the scope of American law, this sentiment is demonstrated by some key cases within the crowd crush issue. Their parallels with the more recent Astroworld tragedy showcase the ongoing nature of the issue.

RELEVANT CASES

Pooser v. Cox Radio, Inc.[312] was a personal injury case in which Appellant Francis Pooser arrived at a rock concert at Verizon Wireless Amphitheater in Selma, Texas under the impression that she would be observing the concert from a designated seat. However, there were no seats and the entire audience was standing in a general admission area colloquially referred to as a "mosh pit."

---

[310] Tracy Hresko Pearl, "Far from the Madding Crowd: A Statutory Solution to Crowd Crush," *Hastings Law Journal* Vol. 68:159 (2016).
[311] John Seabrook, *Crush Point*, Annals of Disaster (Jan. 30, 2011)
https://www.newyorker.com/magazine/2011/02/07/crush-point
[312] Pooser v. Cox Radio, 04-08-00270-CV, (2009)

While in the mosh pit, the crowd caused Pooser to suffer a head injury while in the area. Pooser then sued Cox Radio as an affiliate of the concert, to which Cox Radio responded that they were merely a promoter of the event and had no jurisdiction over Pooser's seat. Legally, The court found that Cox Radio did not have duty in regards to Pooser's ability to find a seat during the concert[313].

Cunningham v. District of Columbia Sports Entertainment Commission[314] was a civil negligence action case brought by plaintiff Justin Cunningham, an attendant at HFStival on May 25, 2002. The festival was headlined by recording artist Eminem and was general admission only. Cunningham and a friend were eager to see Eminem and pushed through the dense crowd to get to the front. Subsequently, the crowd began "moshing," or engaging in actions that involve "pushing, running, throwing, and slamming into each other," and Cunningham's friend got trampled. During Eminem's performance, a police officer testified that he saw a pile of "thirty to fifty bodies." The plaintiff was one of those bodies. The performer stopped the show and instructed the crowd to back up. Cunningham was in a coma for the following six days, suffering from rhabdomyolysis from the crowd crush. The court ruled in favor of Cunningham and ordered that the D.C. SEC provide pay damages[315]. It was found that it was the negligence of the venue organizers and Eminem himself, due to the knowledge that Eminem's concerts tend to contain a fair

---

[313] *Id*

[314] Cunningham v. Dist. of Columbia Sports Entertainment Comm, Civil Action No. 03-839(RWR)(JMF) (D.D.C. Nov. 30, 2005)
[315] *Id*

amount of tumultuousness among the crowd, which lead to Cunningham's injury.

Prettyman v. Trenton Transportation Co. was a personal injury case in which plaintiff Sarah Pretty-man was knocked unconscious by a surging crowd that was attempting to cross a wharf at Burlington Island Park and board an excursion steamboat. The defendant is the owner and operator of the boat. The guiding question of the case was whether or not the defendant had reason to expect the excitement and unruliness of the crowd that led to the plaintiff's injury. It was found that the defendant had no reason to expect this crowd surge and thus did not demonstrate reasonable negligence, so the court ruled in its favor[316].

ANALYSIS

There are substantive ways that the United States legal system and venues themselves can prevent future incidents of crowd crush. In the past, policy has failed to protect audiences across modes of live entertainment. For example, prior to *Cunningham*, there was no duty placed upon the performer to mitigate the risk of a surging crowd, but the case has set a precedent for performers to be held liable for being aware of a dangerous situation but not stopping the show, as Travis Scott is currently under fire for[317]. Additionally, the court system has been hyper focused on capacity numbers, building code compliance, while also placing a

---

[316] Prettyman v. Trenton Transportation Co. 73 Pa. Super. 353 (Feb 28, 1920)

[317] Tracy Hresko Pearl, "Crowd Crush: How the Law Leaves American Crowds Unprotected," Kentucky Law Journal: Vol. 104 : Iss. 1 , Article 4. (2015)

disproportionate amount of blame on the crowd itself[318]. Assumption of risk is also called into question, as venues and promoters have argued that attendees knew the possibility of a violent crowd when attending[319].

Experts suggest that the legal system proceed with recommending crowd density calculations for event hosts, intertwining expert testimony in court proceedings, and, according to Tracy Hresko Pearl, excluding "evidence about official capacity numbers, building code compliance, and the demographic characteristics of individual crowd members."[320] In particular, building code compliance is a compelling legal idea in relation to concerts and their safety. Fire marshal inspections are conducted to ensure the accessibility and clarity of emergency exits as well as other code violations[321].

The lattermost suggestion is especially relevant when discussing concert crowds, as victims are blamed for their injury due to assumptions about their character and conduct, which can be racialized or stereotypical. Also, it is important that planners set out clear routes for attendees to enter, leave, and mobilize within, plan out precise areas that are occupied by the crowds, anticipate the movement of the crowd as the event progresses, understand the crowd demographics and the nature of the event to cater to their needs, monitor the crowd in

---

[318] *Id*

[319] *Id*

[320] *Id*

[321] Office of the Fire Marshal, *Office of the Fire Marshal,* Fire and EMS Operations (n.d.) ttps://fems.dc.gov/page/office-fire-marshal

real time, and ensure clear and streamlined communication.[322]

CONCLUSION

The Astroworld disaster joins a long list of crowd crush incidents with fascinating legal implications. An important nuance is that Scott has a history of creating violent scenarios at his concerts, and Live Nation as well as his team failed to recognize the demographics of Scott's audience as well as Scott's encouragement of such behavior.[323] Given the numerous crowd crush incidents before Astroworld, it is egregious that concert venues have not taken proper action in properly managing crowds per the recommendations of experts. The outcome of the lawsuits filed against Scott and Live Nation will hopefully shape the way entertainment safety and legal accountability progresses in the future. Crowd crush incidents occur too often for there to be no comprehensive reform and insurance of safety for event attendees. Entertainment should not be a deadly affair, and this easily avoidable phenomenon cannot be pinned on the perceived disorderliness of attendees.

---

[322] Tracy Hresko Pearl, "Far from the Madding Crowd: A Statutory Solution to Crowd Crush," *Hastings Law Journal* Vol. 68:159 (2016).
[323] Eliane Aini, "Travis Scott: Is He Responsible for a Disaster "Butterfly E vis Scott: Is He Responsible for a Disaster 'Butterfly Effect'?" *AELJ Blog.* 305.
https://larc.cardozo.yu.edu/aelj-blog/305

THE STAR OF THE SHOW: THE ROLE OF NDA'S IN THE ENTERTAINMENT WORLD

BY MARIANA ESPINOZA

INTRODUCTION

In the media, there has been an increase in the coverage of celebrities who use non-disclosure agreements (NDAs) with their spouses, nannies, friends, family, or even employees. There has also been a debate regarding the efficacy of NDAs and this comes in light of the Me Too movement that occurred in 2017 as a result of sexual assault allegations from Harvey Weinstein. While there are good reasons for having NDAs there are also important issues that should be addressed when an NDA is used inappropriately. Current experts in the field are discussing whether NDAs should no longer be allowed as a contract or whether they can be reformed and follow strict regulations and laws regarding NDAs.

WHAT IS AN NDA?

NDAs are a type of legal contract between at least two parties. The contract is meant to protect the confidentiality of any type of information that was shared between the parties. There are three kinds of NDAs: a unilateral agreement, a bilateral agreement, and a multilateral agreement. A unilateral NDA involves two parties and is a "one-way" agreement where whatever one party says is meant to be protected. A bilateral NDA is where both parties' information is kept confidential and thus protected. A multilateral NDA involves three or more parties where at least one of the various parties is disclosing confidential information to the others.

The interesting thing about NDAs is that no one knows who created them. The earliest record of NDAs being used was in the 1940s in relation to maritime law.[324] Over time NDAs began appearing more often as tech firms started to develop and would want to protect key information like their latest software, any new projects, etc.[325] By the 1980s, NDAs were appearing in all aspects of American society; the business world, the political sphere, and Hollywood.

NDAS IN ENTERTAINMENT

Many celebrities have NDAs not only with their employers but even with friends, family, coworkers, and other people who may interact with them daily. Because celebrities are constantly in the public eye, they are not

---

[324] Jesse Kerema, *What is an NDA? Everything you need to know about NDA's*, Sine (Jan. 28, 2020) https://www.sine.co/blog/nda/

[325] Michelle Dean, Contracts of silence, Columbia Journalism Review. (2018) https://www.cjr.org/special_report/nda-agreement.php#:~:text =There's%20no%20clear%20origin%20story,the%20context% 20of%20maritime%20law.

seen as regular citizens. For this reason, the more famous a person is, the less likely they are entitled to a right to privacy. This is because celebrities' actions are considered to be part of the "public domain" since they're always and oftentimes willingly, in the spotlight.

One of the few Supreme Court cases surrounding publicity is *Zacchini v. Scripps Howard Broadcasting Company* (1977). The case surrounds performer Hugo Zacchini, who would perform his "human cannonball" act. A reporter for Scripps-Broadcasting Co. recorded the performance despite Zacchini telling him not to and it was aired on the nighttime news. The case called to question whether the first and fourteenth amendments protected the broadcasting company from damages done to Zacchini of the alleged unlawful appropriation of his professional property (i.e. his performance).

In a 5-4 decision, the Supreme Court found that the broadcasting company's protected speech did not apply to them broadcasting Zacchini's performance without his consent. It should be noted that the Court said there was a difference between reporting on the event and solely broadcasting the entire performance. Furthermore, the Court focused on the plaintiff's proprietary interest saying, that because the broadcast "pose[d] a substantial threat to the economic value of that performance," the "same consideration underlying the patent and copyright laws" thus protected Zacchini's right to publicity as "an economic incentive for him to make the investment required to produce a performance of interest to the public."[326]

---

[326] Zacchini v. Scripps-Howard Broadcasting Co., 433 U.S. 562, p. 575-76

Looking at modern-day celebrities, because of this priority held over economic interest as opposed to privacy, whenever famous people want to sue someone for releasing their information, as opposed to arguing that it was a violation of privacy, lawyers of celebrities typically argue that the information leaked had some monetary value and as a result, by breaching the confidentiality agreement, caused financial harm/ damage to their client.[327]

This was the case in 2005 when a former nanny of Victoria and David Beckham, Abbie Gibson, violated their confidentiality agreement and went to the tabloids leaking information regarding their personal affairs. Ultimately, the British court ruled in favor of Gibson, arguing that because the Beckhams are public figures by personal choice, the Beckhams didn't have as much of a right to privacy as a regular citizen would.[328] In this case, Paul Nicholas Boylan who specializes in NDAs says that the couple, instead of focusing the argument on privacy, should have argued in terms of protecting financial interests.[329] He says, "The agreement should have stated that they owned all the information about themselves and that such information had monetary value... So if the Beckhams' nanny breached the confidentiality

---

[327] Audrey Davidow, *L.A.'s secret service*, Los Angeles Times (Jul. 26, 2007)
https://www.latimes.com/archives/la-xpm-2007-jul-26-hm-con fidential26-story.htmlhttps://www.latimes.com/archives/la-xp m-2007-jul-26-hm-confidential26-story.html
[328] Audrey Davidow, *L.A.'s secret service*, Los Angeles Times (Jul. 26, 2007)
[329] Audrey Davidow, *L.A.'s secret service*, Los Angeles Times (Jul. 26, 2007)

agreement and sold the information, the nanny would have been stealing from the Beckhams."[330]

AN ANALYSIS OF THE BENEFITS AND DRAWBACKS OF NDAS

With how often NDAs are used both in entertainment and in regular life, there are certainly many benefits. The first is that the information one wants to be kept confidential will be under an NDA. Another benefit is that an NDA clearly stipulates what information is confidential and also limits how the receiving party can use the information elicited (if at all). Because NDAs clearly outline what is and isn't permissible, it also outlines the consequences if the contract is breached. Typically the party that is giving out the information will also stipulate that if the contract is breached then they will file for damages or a type of loss wherein they can be compensated for such damages.[331] These benefits apply to almost every field of work whether it's business, entertainment, etc.

Looking from an entertainment perspective, however, there are also some drawbacks; especially given the attention NDAs have garnered over the past few years. Back when Me Too was gaining traction in 2017, there was a lot of discussion surrounding the NDAs made by the disgraced film producer Harvey Weinstein. Weinstein would use NDAs in his settlements with women who

---

[330] Audrey Davidow, *L.A.'s secret service*, Los Angeles Times (Jul. 26, 2007)
[331] Lauren McKee, *5 Benefits of Using a Non-Disclosure Agreement*, Legal Vision (Feb. 4, 2021) https://legalvision.com.au/5-benefits-of-using-a-non-disclosure-agreement/

accused him of assault. These NDAs would include clauses that would prevent the employee who signed it from talking about Weinstein's "personal, social or business activities."[332] Because employees who sign the NDA would risk being sued if they broke the contract, it's clear that an NDA in instances of sexual harassment and assault is used as a power play by those in the higher chain of command. This has led to a lot of discussion and scrutiny surrounding NDAs. According to experts in the legal field, there is limited case law as to whether or not contractual agreements like NDAs to settle sexual harassment claims can be enforced.[333] For this reason, NDAs are used to intimidate and scare survivors into keeping quiet.

WHAT'S THE VERDICT– ARE NDAS GOOD OR BAD?

While there are some positives and negatives to NDAs, it begs the question: should they still be allowed? The answer isn't one-size-fits-all. Many experts suggest that NDAs should be used in the business realm to prevent trade secrets from being leaked.[334] There are, however, barriers put in place to prevent individuals from abusing NDAs. For example, it was revealed that in 2016 former President Trump had NDAs for everyone who not only

[332] Ronan Farrow, *Harvey Weinstein's Secret Settlements*, The New Yorker (Nov. 21, 2017) https://www.newyorker.com/news/news-desk/harvey-weinsteins-secret-settlements
[333] Nicole Einbinder, *What Happens If Someone Breaks a Non-Disclosure Agreement?*, PBS Frontline (Mar. 2, 2018) https://www.pbs.org/wgbh/frontline/article/what-happens-if-someone-breaks-a-non-disclosure-agreement/
[334] Nicole Einbinder, *What Happens If Someone Breaks a Non-Disclosure Agreement?*, PBS Frontline (Mar. 2, 2018)

worked on his campaign but also worked in the White
House. The NDA defined confidential information that
"Mr. Trump insists remain private or confidential."[335]
However, under the federal Defend Trade Secrets Act
(DTSA), there is a whistle-blower immunity clause. In
2016, when the law was passed, every NDA must
include a paragraph that explains that employees have
whistleblowing rights.[336]

Another protection comes from laws where the
enforceability of confidentiality agreements are done by
state law. But there are certain exceptions wherein
federal statutes are considered. In those instances, there
are federal laws that place limits on nondisclosure
agreements, but some companies may ignore those
limits.[337] States get to decide whether to disregard certain
contractual provisions signed by workers and employers
"as long as no federal law mandates enforcement."[338]
Two types of confidentiality clauses relate to harassment
claims: broad waivers forbidding employees from
expressing any form of speech and a clause where
employees are paid to drop their claims and not speak on
the matter afterward. Broad waivers that forbid

---

[335] Orly Lobel, *Trump's Extreme NDAs*, The Atlantic (Mar. 4,
2019)
https://www.theatlantic.com/ideas/archive/2019/03/trumps-use
-ndas-unprecedented/583984/
[336] Orly Lobel, *Trump's Extreme NDAs*, The Atlantic (Mar. 4,
2019)
[337] Daniel Hemel, *How nondisclosure agreements protect
sexual predators*, Vox (Oct. 13, 2017)
https://www.vox.com/the-big-idea/2017/10/9/16447118/confid
entiality-agreement-weinstein-sexual-harassment-nda
[338] Daniel Hemel, *How nondisclosure agreements protect
sexual predators*, Vox (Oct. 13, 2017)

employees from speaking about any form of harassment goes against the Wagner Act[339], a labor law.[340]

In the aftermath of the Weinstein trials, many experts in the legal field have looked to see if there were any ways that NDAs could be reformed. A law professor at New York University, Samuel Estricher offered the strategy where the Equal Employment Opportunity Commission (EEOC) would keep track of companies that settle sexual harassment cases and investigate companies that repeatedly use NDAsfor the same employees.[341] Another rule that could be implemented is making sure that employees know they have a right to speak with an attorney prior to signing the contract. While many may be a proponent for getting rid of NDAs entirely, law professor at DePaul University, Wendy Netter Epstein says it would give employers less incentive to settle cases. Harassers would thus be able to retaliate against accusers since they are no longer bound by a confidentiality clause. [342]

Many legal experts feel that there are NDAs that are appropriate when used correctly, and then those that aren't. Ultimately, there should be a better system that

---

[339] The Wagner Act of 1935 is meant to establish a worker's legal right to organize and join unions and to bargain with their employers.
[340] Daniel Hemel, *How nondisclosure agreements protect sexual predators*, Vox (Oct. 13, 2017)
[341] Nicole Einbinder, *What Happens If Someone Breaks a Non-Disclosure Agreement?*, PBS Frontline (Mar. 2, 2018) https://www.pbs.org/wgbh/frontline/article/what-happens-if-someone-breaks-a-non-disclosure-agreement/
[342] Nicole Einbinder, *What Happens If Someone Breaks a Non-Disclosure Agreement?*, PBS Frontline (Mar. 2, 2018)

brings clarity and establishes what is and isn't acceptable when it comes to a confidentiality agreement.

CONCLUSION

NDAs have become such a highly used type of contract over the past few decades from the political realm to Hollywood. From its likely inception in the 1940s in maritime law to its adoption in tech firms, NDAs have been used as a means to ensure confidentiality between two or more parties. In relation to the entertainment industry, NDAs have been used by many celebrities to try and protect their privacy rights. Overall, there are many reasons why NDAs should and should not be continued to be used. As was mentioned previously, the main benefit of NDAs is that it protects content, information, and ideas that people want to be private and protected. Despite the positive intent this contract has, there are people who have used NDAs to exploit people and to enable people to take advantage of others. As many have started to recognize how abusive NDAs can be when used incorrectly, legal experts have considered whether or not NDAs should no longer exist or whether they can be reformed to ensure all parties are protected from malice and abusive contracts. These questions will likely be further explored as abusive actions in the entertainment industry are no longer kicked under the rug and performers' rights are protected.

NUDITY CLAUSES AND THE EUPHORIA CASE STUDY

BY SOPHIA OLSON

INTRODUCTION

When it comes to Nudity Clauses, there is no formal legal process or standard. The only legal aspect of the document is the final contract that the parties sign. However, there is no legal ruling that says what this contract has to look like. The contract's details come down to the party's union status, leveraging power, and whether or not a lawyer wrote the contract or not. These are just a few of the factors that go into the contract that is signed that would be the document held up in court if a party believes their contract was violated when it came to their nudity within a film.

CASTING AND NUDITY

When looking at the Sag- AFTRA contract there are a few important things to note.[343] The first is that there is

---

[343] The Screen Actors Guild - American Federation of Television and Radio Artists, Summary of Tentative Agreement: SAG-AFTRA TV/Theatrical Contracts, SAG-AFTRA (2020),

no agreement that allows a producer to request an actor to perform a real sex act. In terms of the audition process. The first part of the audition process requires a clear posting on a casting call that there will be nudity or sex acts, ie simulated sex, in an audition. Nudity is only allowed at a final callback. No matter the case, the use of cameras and recording are strictly prohibited. These are the required standards for those who are considered union actors. If someone is non-union, there is no union contract that requires these stipulations be upheld at auditions.

NUDITY RIDERS

Once one is cast into a role, a contract is written up that outlines the agreed-upon terms of the role and its nudity requirements. Similar to the audition process, there are no required legal boundaries when it comes to nudity and its performance outlined within the contract. Instead, it comes down to what one can negotiate into the contract. This comes from how much power an actor has in the negotiation process. When an actor has power or union membership a common contractual addition is a "Nudity Rider". This requires directors to inform actors of scenes where they will be nude prior to shooting. Nudity Riders are documents that list all times nudity or sex acts will be required in the script.[344] These documents are considered to be the contractual

---

https://www.sagaftra.org/files/sa_documents/SAG-AFTRA_20
20TV-Theatrical_Summary.pdf

[344] Anthony Ferranti, Everything You Ever Wanted to Know about Nudity Clauses but Were Too Shy to Ask, FilmIndependent (2017),
https://www.filmindependent.org/blog/everything-you-ever-w
anted-to-know-about-nudity-clauses-but-were-too-shy-to-ask/

agreement to nudity between director and actor. In cases where there is an added nudity or sex act, the contract must be revisited. However, many SAG-AFTRA members follow the rule that performers must be informed of the scene 48 hours in advance of the call time, and must have the rider amended and signed off on by the performer before completing the act.

FILMED NUDITY

In terms of When the actual scene is being filmed, the ability for a performer to back out of the scene if they feel uncomfortable comes down to what the contract says. For union actors contracts are typically written that the performer reserves the power to back out of filming the scene. In that case, the producer holds the right then to put a body double in place. If an actor decides after filming the scene, the producer holds the full right to use the footage even if the actor objects to the use of it after it is filmed. In a case where the contract does not have a clause on changing one's mind on a nude scene, the dispute would have to be settled in a non-legal manner as there is no contract to support the requirement of nudity, or the ability to step out of a nude scene.[345]

SAG-AFTRA UNION IMPACT

Now all of these are SAG-AFTRA theatrical contract clauses. This means that they apply to actors who are

---

[345] Heather Hruby, That's Show Business Kid: An Overview of Contract Law in the Entertainment Industry, 27 J. Juv. L. 47, 51 (2006), https://heinonline.org/HOL/LandingPage?handle=hein.journal s/jjuvl27&div=7&id=&page=

union members. Therefore if an actor is not in the union, they don't hold the same amount of rights. However, non-union actors can create their own contracts that contain similar nudity clause requirements.

Furthermore, if someone is a member of the SAG-AFTRA union, they will have a business representative that will look over their nudity riders. The representative will make sure the actor understand their rights and help the performer decide what level of nudity, and sex acts they are comfortable putting their written consent down to perform.

At the end of the day, there is no formal or legal standard for how a nudity clause in an actor's contract should be created. The ability to write a contract that reflects an actor's desires comes when an actor has the power, and star power to negotiate a legal contract in the way that they want it to look. A preferable contract could also come from an actor holding union status, giving them negotiating power when it comes to drafting the legal contracts surrounding nudity.

EUPHORIA CASE STUDY

Recently Euphoria Writer and Producer Sam Levinson have come under fire in the press for supposedly making performers uncomfortable in reference to nudity within the show. While there is always a conversation needed around how nudity and power dynamics play out on sets, it is important to understand how the Nudity clause played a role in the scenes of nudity.

Mika Kelly recalled that Levinson thought Kelly should be nude in the scene that introduces her character. However, upon arriving at the set, Kelly realized she was not comfortable with herself being nude in the scene. Instead of being forced to perform a nude scene, Levinson listened to Kelly's desire to stay clothed and did not require her to be nude.

When framing these examples within the idea of nudity clauses, the question comes up of the state of each actor's nudity riders. In the example of Mika Kelly, the question needs to be asked on whether or not an actor was informed ahead of time about the nudity clause. If the actor was informed of the nudity in the scene on arrival, then the contract would need to be referenced in order to understand if it was broken. As seen with the SAG-AFTRA clauses, most union contracts would state that an actor would have been entitled to 48-hour notice.

Secondly, in the case of feeling that it was uncomfortable, the contract would need to be referenced. If there was a clause about a possible body double opportunity, then requiring an actor to do a scene of nudity would be against the nudity clause.

The contract between Kelly and Euphoria and HBO is no public record, so one cannot examine the legality of her request to remain clothed. If she had a contract that required to be nude, and she was given the appropriate notice, she could have been required to complete her contractual requirements. If she did complete them, Levinson and HBO could have sued her for violation of the contract. However, in this case, Levinson immediately agreed to the lack of nudity and continued on. This could mean that Kelly had a nudity clause that allowed her to refuse nudity at any point in the filming process. Two, Kelly did not have a nudity clause, therefore she did not have a requirement to do a nude scene and thus could refuse at any point. Three Kelly had a nudity clause that required her to do the scene, but Levinson decided to agree to Kelly's desires, and did not worry about the legal breakage, as he saw her desire as more important than a contractual breakage. While we cannot know the contractual agreement, we don't know whether or not Kelly broke a contract in her desire to stay clothed, however, we can assume that regardless of the contract or lack thereof, Kelly's desires were respected and she was not required to complete a scene she felt was violating.

In Euphoria, Zendaya plays the lead character. However, in a show of mass amounts of nudity, Zendaya never once is nude. Not even a body double of nudity is used for her character. While one cannot verify that Zendaya had a contract that included an absolutely full stop on nudity, her character's lack of nudity and Zendaya's process of being cast can be used as evidence that she has a deep contract on this. Zendaya was personally sought out as the lead actor of Euphoria. Because Zendaya was in high demand, she had the power to ask for clauses within a contract that appealed to her desires. This means she could ask for a full no nudity clause and get it while also getting the role, whereas actors who simply auditioned for the role instead of being sought out would have less negotiating room and would have to have looser nudity riders.[346]

---

[346] Brain J Pollock, *The Government May Institute a Total Ban on Public Nudity in Order to*
Combat the Secondary Effects Associated With Adult Entertainment Establishments, 11 Seton Hall Const. Law Journal. 151, 161-63 (2000),
https://go.gale.com/ps/i.do?p=AONE&u=googlescholar&id=GALE|A385796309&v=2.1&it=r&sid=AONE&asid=19314f8d

LEGALITY OF NUDITY CLAUSES

As you read this paper you may be wondering why there are no legal sources. That is because there is no legal precedent for what nudity clauses need to look like for tv and film contracts. Instead, contracts are made based on negotiations that are based on power dynamics, creative control, and artist advocates. Because the lines are so gray when it comes to nudity clauses, the exploitation and events highlighted in recent #MeToo movements are far too common, and far too persecuted due to legal failings.

To solve the harms done due to sexual exploitation, we need to make stronger legal presidents for nudity clauses and stronger legal ramifications for exploitative practices within nudity clauses. Once we begin to have conversations around creating these legal presidents, we can make a safer film and television sector.

CONCLUSION

The legality of nudity within film and television comes down to the contract that a performer is able to draft with a studio and lawyers. The amount of nudity that an actor prefers, and the amount required from them within a contract comes down to how much power said performer has. Star power, the director's desire for a specific performer, and union status all influence what a contract looks like, and how it reflects a performer's comfort level of nudity.

THE AMERICAN UNIVERSITY
UNDERGRADUATE LAW JOURNAL

AU UNDERGRAD
LAW JOURNAL

IMMIGRATION

AND

INTERNATIONAL

LAW

COLUMN

THE CASE AGAINST BIG OIL

BY ETHAN GASKILL

INTRODUCTION

Since the end of World War II and the military tribunals conducted in Nuremberg and Tokyo, the United Nations has been the chief international authority when it comes to formulating responses to atrocities, as defined in the Geneva Conventions, their additional protocols, and the Rome Statute. In the 1990s, several tribunals were convened by the UN Security Council with the mandate of trying the leaders of various countries with crimes against humanity related to their actions during the Yugoslav wars, Rwandan genocide, Sierra Leone Civil War, and the Cambodian genocide.

In 2002 the International Criminal Court ("the Court") was established. In the Rome Statute, the founding document of the ICC, there are four crimes which are established to be under the jurisdiction of the Court. They are the crime of genocide, war crimes, the crime of aggression, and crimes against humanity[347]. Since its

---

[347] Rome Statute of the International Criminal Court, Pt. 2 Art. 5

establishment, the ICC has served as an investigative body for cases referred to it by the UN Security Council[348]. The Court's definition of crimes against humanity, which is the broadest definition of the term in international law to date, includes "inhumane acts of a similar character intentionally causing great suffering, or serious injury to body or to mental or physical health"[349]. Despite knowing that the consumption of fossil fuels would put the planet in grave jeopardy and harm the physical and mental health of vulnerable populations around the globe, executives of the major petroleum companies proceeded to promote their product. Considering the Court's definition of crimes against humanity, it is clear that executives of the world's major petroleum corporations have intentionally and negligently committed crimes against humanity through putting the physical health of the world's population in serious jeopardy and through the bodily harm that has already occurred as a result of their business practices.

PURPOSEFUL IGNORANCE OF SCIENCE

In 1961 British meteorologist Charles Keeling published the Keeling Curve, which visualized data he collected from 1958-1960 which showed rapidly increasing levels of carbon dioxide in the atmosphere[350]. Despite the fact that the combustion of fossil fuels was known to release carbon dioxide into the atmosphere, and that scientists had determined increased levels of CO_2 to be

---

[348] https://www.icc-cpi.int/pages/situation.aspx
[349] Rome Statute of the International Criminal Court, Pt. 2 Art. 7, Clause 1k
[350]

https://www.upsbatterycenter.com/blog/climate-change-part-12-the-keeling-curve/

responsible for rising temperatures, the Keeling Curve initially received little to no attention from his scientific peers upon its release, although it did eventually receive acclaim[351].

By 1977, at least one major petroleum company was aware of the scientific research demonstrating a correlation between the combustion of fossil fuels, rising levels of atmospheric carbon dioxide, and a trend of global warming.

According to an investigation conducted by InsideClimate News and published in Scientific American, in July 1977 senior Exxon scientist James Black told the company's management committee, "In the first place, there is general scientific agreement that the most likely manner in which mankind is influencing the global climate is through carbon dioxide release from the burning of fossil fuels." Black then continued to tell them that "present thinking holds that man has a time window of five to 10 years before the need for hard decisions regarding changes in energy strategies might become critical."[352] With the knowledge we have now in 2022, it is clear to see that Exxon did not act on this knowledge. As we see first hand the negative consequences that this inaction is having on the health of our planet and our fellow man, it becomes clear that this inaction is tantamount to criminal negligence.

351

https://science.anu.edu.au/news-events/news/how-we-disco
vered-climate-problem

352

https://www.scientificamerican.com/article/exxon-knew-about
-climate-change-almost-40-years-ago/

During the Nuremberg Tribunals, Friedrich Krupp AG CEO Gustav Krupp von Bohlen und Halbach and his son were indicted for crimes against humanity for his company's use of slave labor during the World War II, as well as the role they played in German rearmament in violation of the Treaty of Versailles. In a 1945 New York Times article, it was also expressed that the indictment of Krupp was seen as "symbolic of all industrialists aiding in incitement to aggressive warfare".[353]

Past military tribunals have shown that business executives can be held responsible when the companies under their control commit crimes against humanity. And while there has not been an ICC proceeding of this nature since the court's inception in 2002, the UN Security Council's past referral of German industrialists for prosecution and the fact that the Security Council still maintains the ability to refer situations to the prosecutor for investigation means that the leaders of major petroleum companies can and should be referred to the Court for investigation today.

These companies' violations of the statutes against crimes against humanity are two pronged: one violation stems from the physical harm caused to humans as a result of their knowing inaction, and another stems from the grave peril the planet is in as a result of their inaction.

With regards to the physical health effects of climate change as a consequence of the continued use of fossil fuels, there is evidence in support of the conclusion that

---

353

https://timesmachine.nytimes.com/timesmachine/1945/11/13/3 05803642.html?pageNumber=1 many different ailments have become more common as a result of climate change. According to a 2005 study that analyzed the increasing prevalence of asthma around the world, "the hypothesis that the global rise of asthma is an early impact of anthropogenic climate change...stands." This study found that the increase in both prevalence and severity of asthma in recent decades "has been far too rapid to implicate any genetic basis for change," which leaves environmental factors as the chief culprit.[354]

With regards to the future peril that the planet faces, consider the recent report from the Intergovernmental Panel on Climate Change. According to its findings, "global warming, reaching 1.5°C in the near-term, would cause unavoidable increases in multiple climate hazards and present multiple risks to ecosystems and humans"[355]. Increases in global temperatures will continue to cause increased rates of asthma, heat stroke, and extreme weather, as well as fundamentally changing the nature of the agricultural industry which supports the world's population. They also added that in the near future, the number of people in danger from climate change and the corresponding loss in biodiversity will progressively increase[356]. When this happens, it will be the direct result of the decision made by executives from petroleum companies not to act on their knowledge of climate change. Their lack of action, despite knowing what would occur as a result of their inaction, and continued efforts to publicly undermine what they privately knew to be true about their product, constitutes a willing

---

[354] https://ehp.niehs.nih.gov/doi/full/10.1289/ehp.7724
[355] https://www.ipcc.ch/report/ar6/wg2/ SPM.B.3
[356] https://www.ipcc.ch/report/ar6/wg2/ SPM.B.3.1

exacerbation of the problem, and of the harm caused to their fellow men.[357]

THE PLAYERS

Because the original evidence of oil executives' knowledge that climate science showed their product to be harmful dates back to 1977, and the leadership of the major oil companies from those times are no longer alive, the question arises of who is legally culpable for the inaction of decades past? Current CEOs might not be solely responsible for the past decisions of their companies, but under the definition provided above, their culpability stems from the fact that they have not acted to correct their course of action.

The refusal of the executives of major oil companies to act to mitigate the effect that their actions would have on global warming was not a one time decision made in 1977. Instead, since they first learned that their actions were responsible for rising temperatures oil companies have engaged in a public disinformation campaign to downplay the scientific conclusions behind climate change.[358] They have deliberately chosen to attempt to shift the blame away from themselves instead of changing their ways. Because of these acts, the current executives of major oil companies are just as responsible for the harm their companies have done to the environment as their predecessors.

---

[357]https://www.nbcnews.com/business/business-news/big-oil-ceos-deny-lying-public-climate-change-rcna4033
[358]

https://www.theguardian.com/environment/2021/nov/18/the-forgotten-oil-ads-that-told-us-climate-change-was-nothing

The three individuals identified below were selected for prosecution based on multiple factors. As established in the Krupp Trial, where the defendants were indicted partially to symbolize the many German industrialists who contributed to the war effort, a prosecution can have symbolic meaning in addition to its primary rationale of punishing those who are legally culpable for a wrong. With this in mind the individuals identified below were selected both because of their leadership of the world's biggest oil companies and to accurately represent the global scope of their crimes.

While many crimes against humanity are categorized as such because the act in question is considered so cruel and transgressive that it is a crime against humanity itself, the crimes that these men committed quite literally make victims of all humanity. Thus, it would be wrong to indict only the leadership from the American oil companies, or any other individual company. The harm caused by these crimes has been the consequence of the acts of oil companies from around the world, and the defendants should be chosen in a similar manner.

With this in mind, the first people identified for indictments should be the leaders of Saudi Aramco, which is the largest oil company in the world measured by market capitalization. Amin Hassan Nasser, the current CEO of Saudi Aramco, and Yasir bin Othman Al-Rumayyan, the chairman of the board of Saudi Aramco. Under the leadership of these two men, Saudi Aramco has been the world leader in supplying oil to the world and has exacerbated the harm done to the planet as a result of their business[359]. Additionally, the fact that SaudiAramco is owned by the Saudi Arabian crown means that the royal family may have exposure to legal culpability as well.

The second group of people who should be held responsible consists of Zhou Jiping, the chairman of PetroChina, and Wang Dongjin, the CEO. Similarly to the leaders of SaudiAramco, the leaders of PetroChina have contributed to the continued use of fossil fuels in the world economy, and are actively taking steps to ensure that developing nations in Africa and Asia are forced to rely on PetroChina to help continue their economic growth, reducing the chance to introduce renewable energy to these nations at the beginning of their industrialization[360]. Similarly to the situation with SaudiAramco and the Saudi Arabian crown, PetroChina's status as a state-owned enterprise could also expose the Chinese state to legal culpability as well.

Finally there is Darren Woods, the American chairman and CEO of ExxonMobil. As the largest American oil company, ExxonMobil's continued operations and past involvement in withholding the truth of climate change from the public earns them a spot on the list. Mr. Woods' own involvement in Exxon's role in this crisis is well documented, as he has personally been accused of lying to Congress about his knowledge relating to ExxonMobil's internal covering-up of climate change

---

[359]

https://www.aramco.com/en/who-we-are/our-corporate-govern ance/corporate-management/amin-h-nasser

[360]

https://www.chinavitae.com/biography/Zhou_Jiping%7c2826

data[361]. As the US economy plays a key role in the continued use of fossil fuels, the largest American oil company must be held responsible for their role in exacerbating the already existing crisis. As the world's fourth largest oil company, and the largest oil company in the United States, ExxonMobil has also done its part to damage the health of the world.

CONCLUSION

The international community and the ICC have a decision to make. The scientific community overwhelmingly believes that not only is climate change an existential threat to humanity, but that people are already suffering physical consequences because of it. The question is not whether or not it is happening, but whether or not there will be repercussions for those responsible.

By indicting the leaders of Saudi Aramco, PetroChina, and ExxonMobil with charges of crimes against humanity stemming from their actions carried out while leading their companies, the Court has the opportunity to take tangible action to begin to hold those in power responsible for their actions. At this advanced stage in the climate crisis, the only viable steps to take are drastic ones. Indicting the leading energy suppliers of the world will undoubtedly have immediate economic and political repercussions, but doing so will also show that the international community is taking the threat of climate change seriously and that everyone responsible, regardless of their national origin or connections to those

---

361

https://www.theguardian.com/environment/2021/oct/28/exxon-ceo-accused-lying-climate-science-congressional-panel in power, will be held accountable to putting humanity in this perilous position.

A COMPREHENSIVE HISTORY AND ANALYSIS OF THE LEGAL CAUSE AND INTERNATIONAL LAWS OF THE PROSECUTION OF WAR AND THEIR INEQUALITY

BY BEN MERMEL

War has been, since the dawn of the human age, the final preferential end state for international disputes. Accordingly, international law has evolved to accommodate the practice, which is both barbaric and yet seems to be central to our civilization. Historically, the vast majority of international law, a large portion of which was written in the past century, has dealt with the regulation of such disputes between sovereign states, but it was not until recently that a majority of recognized nations came together in concert to codify a unified body of international law. Inherent to this body of law are tenets regarding both the initiation as well as prosecution of said wars.

INTRODUCTION

In the modern era, under the internationally recognized system of international governance created at the end of the Second World War,[362] a nation requires not only a moral, strategic, or economic justification to initiate a conflict, but a legal one as well. The United Nations,[363] the central governing authority on matters of international law lists in its founding charter only three such legal justifications: self defense, the defense of an ally when required by compact or treaty, and the express assent of the United Nations[364]. These causes are and have been collectively known to the international community legally as *casus belli*, literally translated as "occasion for war."[365] A related concept referred to here earlier is *casus foederis,* or "cause for alliance."[366] Both of these concepts form the basis of a state's legal right to declare war. In addition, states must conduct themselves in an equitable and proportional manner when prosecuting a war, including treating combatants fairly and preserving the lives of non-combatants. However, these rules are not the same for all, and are in many cases, applied unequally.

THE HISTORY OF INTERNATIONAL LAW

---

[362] John Graham Royde-Smith, World War II Encyclopedia Britannica (2022), https://www.britannica.com/event/World-War-II (last visited Apr 7, 2022)

[363] Jacques Fomerand, United Nations Encyclopedia Britannica (2020), https://www.britannica.com/topic/United-Nations (last visited Apr 7, 2022)

[364] United Nations Charter, United Nations Conference on International Organization (1945).

[365] Casus belli, Merriam-Webster

[366] Casus foederis, Merriam-Webster

Understanding the history of international law is key to understanding it. Many of the concepts that are central to international law originate within texts and teachings of philosophers and thinkers throughout history. As the individuals who composed contemporary international law drew heavily upon these figures, it is necessary to discuss where and how those ideas were developed. The history of international law is long and storied, and developments in the field were both vertical and lateral in nature, with successive thinkers building on what came before, all the way up until the modern codified body of international law.

Throughout history, states have sought a mechanism for resolving disputes and regulating the conduct of armed forces in war. The evolution of this mechanism, for much of history lies in philosophy, and the very first step came in the form of a recognition of states as discrete entities. In the earliest sense, bipolar agreements existed between city-states as far back as the 2nd millennium B.C., such as the compact between the cities of Lagaš and Uruk in ancient Mesopotamia regulating the dual hegemony of the time, as iterated on a clay nail of King Entemena of Lagaš,[367] [368]stating - "For Inanna and Lugal-emuš Enmetena, ruler of Lagaš, the E-muš, their beloved temple, built and ordered (these) clay nails for them. Enmetena, who built the E-muš, his personal god is Šul-utul. At that time, Enmetena, ruler of Lagaš, and Lugal-kineš-dudu, ruler of Uruk, *established brotherhood*." Historically, this is most likely the first, or

---

[367] Deena Ragavan, Cuneiform Digital Library Journal CDLJ 2010:1 (2010), https://cdli.ucla.edu/pubs/cdlj/2010/cdlj2010_001.html (last visited Apr 5, 2022).

[368] Editors of Encyclopedia Britannica , Lagash Encyclopedia Britannica (2009), https://www.britannica.com/place/Lagash (last visited Apr 6, 2022)

one of the first instances of diplomatic law being formally enshrined in the form of a treaty between two entities. Further along through the ages, the concept of war and "just war" became developed by philosophers of China, Greece, and India.

Beyond the identification of two discrete identities, an inherent prerequisite for diplomacy, there lies the identification of those empowered to parley diplomatically; those individuals that possess effective command authority. In China, thinkers influenced by Kǒngzǐ[369] (孔子), anglicized as Confucius[370], analyzed the nature of war as it related to the fundamental tenets of absolute monarchy, electing to determine that war was only to be declared upon three conditions; firstly, that war be utilized as a last resort, secondly, that war may only be declared by the sovereign, and finally, that the inherent "right" of the war be hinged upon the efficacy of its prosecution. There then came a principle of fairness, not attributed to any specific origin, merely a recognition of its existence. In India, both Hindu and Sikh writers alike recognized that not only must the cause of war be justified, but the manner in which it is conducted must also be equitable, and the weapons used must kill in a comparatively humane way. Vyasa[371], the

---

[369] Mark Cartwright, Confucius World History Encyclopedia (2012), https://www.worldhistory.org/Confucius/ (last visited Apr 6, 2022).
[370] Karl F. Friday, *The Meaning of War*, *in* Samurai, warfare and the state in early medieval Japan (2010).
[371] The Editors of Encyclopedia Britannica, Vyasa Encyclopedia Britannica (2017), https://www.britannica.com/biography/Vyasa (last visited Apr 6, 2022).

THE AMERICAN UNIVERSITY
UNDERGRADUATE LAW JOURNAL

sage, and the most likely author of the Bhishma Parva[372] of the Mahabharata[373] expressed that -

> Those who engaged in a battle of words should be fought against with only words. Those that left the fight should never be killed. A car-warrior should fight only with a car-warrior. He who rode on an elephant should fight only with another such combatant ..., a horse man must fight with a horse man and a foot-soldier with a foot-soldier. Always being led by consideration of fitness, willingness, bravery and strength, one should strike another after having challenged him. None should strike another who is confiding or who is panic-stricken. One fighting with another, one seeking refuge, one retreating, one whose weapon is broken and one who is not clad in armor should never be struck. Charioteers, animals, men engaged in carrying weapons, those who play on drums and those who blow conches should never be smitten.

These tenets outline a highly developed code, and while it may be mythological in nature, the passage, written around two thousand years ago, defines the principle of proportional response, dictates the treatment of those who surrender, and the inviolability of certain support personnel such as logisticial specialists. Concurrently, the Sikh concept of Dharamyudh[374] illustrated that conflict is permissible to initiate only when threatened,

---

[372] Vyasa, in Mahabharata - Bhishma Parva (Kisari Mohan Ganguli tran., 1990).

[373] Wendy Doniger, Mahabharata Encyclopedia Britannica (2020), https://www.britannica.com/topic/Mahabharata (last visited Apr 6, 2022).

[374] Louis E. Fenech & W. H. McLeod, *Dharam-Yudh*, in Historical Dictionary of Sikhism (2014).

and all possible peaceful methods of egress have been attempted.

When discussing the principle of fairness, and seeking an origin, it follows that a thinker may turn to the observable world to place a rationale - nature and by concurrence, the law of nature. In the Western tradition, Aristotle of Athens initially posited in *Politics*,[375] rejecting the kratocratic[376] theory of "might makes right," that - "The proper object of practising military training is not in order that men may enslave those who do not deserve slavery, but in order that first they may themselves avoid becoming enslaved to others." This constitutes a differing rationale, one where the principles of fairness are applied not to the conduct of war, nor its initiation, but rather explicitly prescribed purely in terms of self-defense to prevent not merely attack, but specifically conquest. However, it is important to note that Aristotle, and indeed many Greek philosophers not only were apathetic to slavery, but openly endorsed the practice, the key term within Aristotle's phrasing being "deserve." This strand of law came about as the natural evolution of the Greco-Roman precept of natural law, or *lex naturalis*[377], which holds that all humans are endowed with particular unalienable rights, a conclusion reached after observation of the natural world. Unalienable natural rights as developed by Aristotle[378]

---

[375] Aristotle & David Keyt, *Book 7* , *in* Politics 1333b (1999).
[376] Dagobert D. Runes, *Kraterocracy*, *in* The Dictionary of Philosophy (1942).
[377] *Jus Naturales in* Merriam-Webster, https://www.merriam-webster.com/dictionary/jus%20naturales (last visited Apr 6, 2022).
[378] Aristotle, *1.13*, *in* Rhetoric (W. Rhys Roberts tran., n.d.), http://www.bocc.ubi.pt/pag/Aristotle-rhetoric.pdf (last visited Apr 6, 2022).

and his followers primarily revolved around the observation of an extant system generally, not in terms of a codified enumerated listing of rights contained within; that there are consequences to actions, and that there was a unified structure regulating these consequences as they related to those actions. Similarly, but slightly set apart, the Stoics, followers of the teachings of Zeno of Citium[379], believed that there was a system, but that the question of that system's existence was immaterial when discussing its origin, divine or anthropogenic. Rather, the *rationality* of the system was more central to its logic, and the argument was made that keeping with the natural order of things was a goal to be desired. This Grecian exploration was applied not only regarding the conduct of humans, but additionally to states piloted by humans, developing into a standard of moral international conduct as wars such as the Peloponnesian War and Phillip II[380] of Macedonia's wars conflagration into existence. Special attention was paid by historians such as Thucydides[381] to the casus belli of those conflicts in texts such as the *History of the Peloponnesian War*,[382] where the rationale for armed disputes like those between the Athenian Empire and Sparta was examined.

---

[379] Editors of Encyclopedia Britannica , Zeno of Citium Encyclopedia Britannica (2022), Zeno of Citium, https://www.britannica.com/biography/Zeno-of-Citium (last visited Apr 6, 2022).

[380] Editors of Encyclopedia Britannica , Phillip II Encyclopedia Britannica (2020), https://www.britannica.com//summary/Philip-II-king-of-Macedonia (last visited Apr 6, 2022).

[381] Arnold Wycombe Gomme , Thucydides Encyclopedia Britannica (2020), https://www.britannica.com/biography/Thucydides-Greek-historian (last visited Apr 6, 2022).

[382] Thucydides, History of the Peloponnesian War (~400 BCE).

Natural law had formed the basis for the principle of equitable conduct up until this point, but had not yet been separated from the laws of man conclusively - what is termed here "civil law." Centuries later, this concept would be expanded upon by scholars such as Gaius, (not to be confused with Gaius Julius Caesar) who molded the Roman concept of *ius gentium*[383], or the "law of nations." In his *Institutes*[384], a commentary on current legal bodies of the time, Gaius lays out that this "law of nations" is the natural evolution of inter (civil law) and intra personal natural law, stating that - "and what natural reason establishes among all men and is observed by all peoples alike, is called the Law of Nations, as being the law which all nations employ." Opening further on this elevated concept of law between communities, the famed philosopher Marcus Tullius Cicero[385], writing in the third volume of his seminal text *De offiiciis*,[386] asserts that due to humanity's nature tending to possess itself of community, and this is what draws the distinction between laws between people (civil law), and laws between communities. He writes -

> This bond of union is closer between those who belong to the same nation and more intimate still between those who are citizens of the same city-state.

---

[383] Ius Gentium, *in* The Oxford Classical Dictionary (Barry Nicholas tran.,).

[384] Gaius, *1.1*, *in* The Institutes (William L. Carey tran., n.d.), http://thelatinlibrary.com/law/gaius1.html (last visited Apr 6, 2022).

[385] John P.V. Dacre Balsdon, Cicero Encyclopedia Britannica (2021), https://www.britannica.com/biography/Cicero (last visited Apr 6, 2022).

[386] Marcus Tullius Cicero, *17*, 3 *in* De Officiis 339–340 (Walter Miller tran., 1913), https://archive.org/details/deofficiiswithen00ciceuoft/page/338/mode/2up?q=17 (last visited Apr 6, 2022).

It is for this reason that our forefathers chose to understand one thing by universal law and another by civil law. The civil law is not necessarily also the universal law.

Finally, Gnaeus Domitius Annius Ulpianus (Ulpian)[387] and Hermogenianus[388] codified the principles of international law as they saw it to fit the instruments of religion and the state, fleshing out the different branches of diplomatic law, and establishing faults and remedies. Respectively, Ulpian divided the law of his time in the first ever instance, into three categories, civil, international, and natural, whilst Hermogenianus[389] delineates within the law of nations subcategories such as war, primogeniture, and colonies. The Romans considered war to be a highly ritualized affair, combining their pantheon and religious practices with matters of the state. This required a theocratic class of priests, labeled as *fetials*,[390] to authorize the conflict by appealing to Jupiter,[391] head of the Roman Pantheon and god of the sky and thunder. These fetials served additionally as Rome's diplomatic staff, performing ambassadorial tasks internationally upon the initiation or

[387] Editors of Encyclopedia Britannica , Ulpian Encyclopedia Britannica (2022), https://www.britannica.com/biography/Ulpian (last visited Apr 6, 2022).
[388] Tony Honoré, Aurelius Hermogenianus Oxford Classical Dictionary, https://www.oxfordreference.com/view/10.1093/oi/authority.2011080 3095932873 (last visited Apr 6, 2022).
[389] Aurelius Hermogenianus, *in* Codex Hermogenianus (293-4AD).
[390] Fetial, Merriam-Webster, https://www.merriam-webster.com/dictionary/fetial (last visited Apr 6, 2022).
[391] Editors of Encyclopedia Britannica , Jupiter (Roman God) Encyclopedia Britannica (2021), Jupiter, https://www.britannica.com/topic/Jupiter-Roman-god (last visited Apr 6, 2022).

conclusion of warfare. This was one of the first instances of a formal order of diplomats, or a commissioned civil service. These views on natural law persisted, particularly when aligned with religion.

In the eyes of religious philosophers, natural law and religion often overlapped, leading to interesting conclusions about morality and war. The Roman Empire became Christianized[392] around the year 45 A.D., and this conversion played a heavy role in the development of what was considered fair in war. Christianity, which had spread from a small corner of Judea, now encompassed a sizable majority of the Roman Empire. The Emperor Constantine I[393], widely thought to have been responsible for the popularity of the new religion, was not, but rather was responsible for issuing, along with Emperor Galerius[394], a series of decrees which prohibited its repression - the Edicts of Toleration[395] and Milan[396]. The rise of Christianity allowed for theological

[392] Rodney Stark, *Chapter 1 / The Arithmetic of Growth*, in The Rise of Christianity: A Sociologist Reconsiders History 4–12 (2021), https://books.google.com/books?id=HcFSaGvgKKkC&printsec=fron tcover&source=gbs_ge_summary_r&cad=0#v=onepage&q=constanti ne&f=false (last visited Apr 6, 2022).
[393] Editors of Encyclopedia Britannica , Constantine I Encyclopedia Britannica (2022), Constantine I, https://www.britannica.com/biography/Constantine-I-Roman-empero r (last visited Apr 6, 2022).
[394] Editors of Encyclopedia Britannica , Galerius Encyclopedia Britannica (2022), Galerius, https://www.britannica.com/biography/Galerius (last visited Apr 6, 2022).
[395] Edward Gibbon, *in* The History of the Decline and Fall of the Roman Empire 132-133 (2008), https://books.google.com/books?id=pksA7j6ZXLgC&pg=PA132#v= onepage&q&f=false (last visited Apr 6, 2022).
[396] Lactantius, *48*, *in* Of the Manner in Which the Persecutors Died 114–118 (Sir David Dalrymple tran., 1782),

scholars such as Saint Augustine of Hippo[397] and Thomas Aquinas[398] to build off of this early thought and develop a new synthesis of personal conduct and legal justification for war. Augustine thought himself a pacifist, and taught that all should strive for pacifism. However, Augustine recognized that pacifism, much like tolerance, must be preserved by selective rejection; that to enable pacifism to thrive, it is sometimes necessary to take up arms to defend it. He refers to this explicitly as a "just war," in his book *The City of God*[399], drawing a comparison between God's first judgment of sin and the judgements made by belligerents - "For even when we wage a just war, our adversaries must be sinning; and every victory, even though gained by wicked men, is a result of the first judgment of God, who humbles the vanquished either for the sake of removing or of punishing their sins." In this, Augustine reveals that he views there to be a calculus, one determined at the onset of conflict, one where an entity must weigh whether there has been harm done, and if it requires rectification. He further elaborates that thought there is a strict religious prohibition against killing, he interprets it to mean *murder*, regarding killing as directed by a legitimate authority to be justified. As he writes[400] -

https://dl.tufts.edu/concern/pdfs/6d570848b (last visited Apr 6, 2022).

[397] James O'Donnell, St. Augustine Encyclopedia Britannica, https://www.britannica.com/biography/Saint-Augustine (last visited Apr 6, 2022).

[398] St Thomas Aquinas, *in* Oxford Reference Dictionary

[399] Aurelius Augustinus Hipponensis, *15*, 1 *in* The City of God 635 (Marcus Dods ed., 1871), https://www.acatholic.org/wp-content/uploads/2014/06/The-City-of-God-Saint-Augustine.pdf (last visited Apr 6, 2022).

[400] Aurelius Augustinus Hipponensis, *20 in* The City of God, https://web.archive.org/web/20130725190746/http://etext.lib.virginia.edu/etcbin/toccer-new2?id=AugCity.xml&images=images%2Fmoden

> They who have waged war in obedience to the divine
> command, or in conformity with His laws, have
> represented in their persons the public justice or the
> wisdom of government, and in this capacity have put
> to death wicked men; such persons have by no means
> violated the commandment, "Thou shalt not kill."

Augustine clearly here identifies that there are those
deserving of offensive action, reconciling it with his
religious principles by alleging a harm to be rectified.

This principle of outlining set justifications for war was
built upon by Augustine's successor, Thomas Aquinas,
who hundreds of years later in the thirteenth century,
would build off of this principle by exploring the
question of what criteria may constitute a just war in his
magnum opus *Summa Theologica,*[401] opting to list them
as -

> "In order for a war to be just, three things are
> necessary. First, the authority of the sovereign by
> whose command the war is to be waged. For it is not
> the business of a private individual to declare war,
> because he can seek redress of his rights from the
> tribunal of his superior. Moreover it is not the
> business of a private individual to summon together
> the   people,   which   has   to   be   done   in
> wartime...Secondly, a just cause is required, namely

---

g&data=%2Ftexts%2Fenglish%2Fmodeng%2Fparsed&tag=public&
part=all (last visited Apr 6, 2022).
[401] Thomas Aquinas, *Q.40*, 2 *in* Summa Theologica (Fathers of the
English Dominican Province tran., 2007),
https://www.newadvent.org/summa/3040.htm (last visited Apr 6,
2022).

that those who are attacked, should be attacked because they deserve it on account of some fault. Wherefore Augustine says -

""A just war is wont to be described as one that avenges wrongs, when a nation or state has to be punished, for refusing to make amends for the wrongs inflicted by its subjects, or to restore what it has seized unjustly."...it is necessary that the belligerents should have a rightful intention, so that they intend the advancement of good, or the avoidance of evil.""

In writing these principles, Aquinas becomes one of the first philosophers to attempt to codify a series of conditions that must be met for a war to be considered justified, a step not yet taken by many in the field. He additionally delineates the responsibilities of the sovereign and the private citizen respectively, and assigns them roles, providing for an early, not yet seen form of an effective command authority. Previously, philosophers and thinkers had agreed that there were differences between just and unjust wars, and sovereign authority to declare them and not, but as yet had not been so clear about the qualifications of a declaration or drawn such clear lines between the role of the sovereign and the people, respectively. Aquinas states that not only must the sovereign declare a war, but the war must be restorative in nature, responding to harm, and finally, the participants must have these just goals during the entire prosecution of such a war. Aquinas here ascribes a "good" and an "evil," terms which fit his unique worldview, but when applied specifically to his answer on the question of war, can be interpreted as conditions that meet the parameters he has specified constitute a just war. Aquinas in turn influenced not just future philosophers, but statesmen as well, far beyond his lifespan.

Developing further this codification of justifications for the cause of war were those that sought to expand upon Augustine and Aquinas' work. A foundational construction for these future statesmen and philosophers that worked directly off of Aquinus' writings was the work of the School of Salamanca[402], a gathering of Spaniard theologians that sought to refine his teachings and apply them to the current foreign and domestic affairs of the nascent Spanish Empire. The conclusions reached by the School were primarily related to casus belli. These critiques arose as a direct result of the Spanish invasion and colonization of the Americas and were as follows: war was permissible in self defense, preventatively in the case of imminent danger, and as penance for a perceived harm. However, they took the important step of not merely regarding a war as just because the purpose at the outset was just, but they additionally required that the purpose be just during the whole affair, fleshing out the sentiment that Aquinas had first offered in *Summa Theologica*. Most importantly perhaps, they recognized the specific rights of the people in adjudicating what constitutes a just war, morally permitting the people to rise up should their leaders enter into an unjust conflict. In particular, one individual thinker by the name of Francisco de Vitoria,[403] one of

---

[402] Thomas Izbicki & Matthias Kaufmann, School of Salamanca Stanford Encyclopedia of Philosophy (2019),
https://plato.stanford.edu/entries/school-salamanca/ (last visited Apr 7, 2022).

[403] Bernice Margaret Hamilton, Francisco de Vitoria Encyclopedia Britannica (2021),
https://www.britannica.com/biography/Francisco-de-Vitoria (last visited Apr 6, 2022).

two persons commonly nicknamed the "father of international law," used the teachings of Aquinas to subvert the Spanish Hapsburg conquest of the New World, arguing that Spain's justification of slavery as posited in Aristitotalian nature was morally bereft and barbaric when applied to the Americas' native population. Victoria's work is known only from lecture notes recorded by his students, but they are respected authorities nonetheless. He laid out his fundamental tenet of inviolability of sovereignty in a lecture presented on the rights of Native Americans[404], stating -

> The upshot of all the preceding is, then, that the aborigines undoubtedly had true dominion in both public and private matters, just like Christians, and that neither their princes nor private persons could be despoiled of their property on the ground of their not being true owners. It would be harsh to deny to those, who have never done any wrong, what we grant to Saracens and Jews, who are the persistent enemies of Christianity. We do not deny that these latter peoples are true owners of their property, if they have not seized lands elsewhere belonging to Christians.

In this, and three following lectures, Vitoria articulates the first recognition of a justification required of conquest as it relates to national sovereignty, and establishes the qualifications for such a determination, whereas those that came before examined only the justification, failing to explicitly consider the assaulted party as an equal entity, legally or otherwise. Vitoria additionally elocuted that the defense of free commerce

---

[404] Francisco de Vitoria et al., *Section 1.24*, *in* Francisco de Vitoria de Indis et de Ivre Belli Relectiones 128 (1917), https://archive.org/details/franciscidevicto0000vito/page/128/mode/2 up?q=upshot (last visited Apr 7, 2022).

was a justifiable reason for waging war, recognizing in a codified way that economic warfare does indeed constitute warfare. Finally, he laid the modern foundations of legal traditions such as that of international waters and the collective ownership of natural resources not in the territory of declared entities.

If Vitoria was the foundation for modern international law, then the superstructure must have been constructed by Huig de Groot (Grotius)[405], a Dutch scholar who followed a century later, and the other individual worthy of the title "father of international law." Grotius' most famed work, and the one that most persists in usage today is his *On the Law of War and Peace*, a treatise on multipolar international security in an age where large and devastating wars often took place. The book was dedicated to King Louis XII of France, who colonized much of North Africa and Canada, and was a patron of Grotius. The book built off of the traditions of all those who came before, including Alberico Gentili[406], and Italian-British scholar who crystalized many of the theories that Grotius built off of, but never received credit. Grotius wrote in *On the Law of War and Peace*[407]

> Fully convinced...that there is a common law among nations, which is valid alike for war and in war, I have had many and weighty reasons for undertaking

---

[405] Jon Miller, Hugo Grotius Stanford Encyclopedia of Philosophy (2005), https://plato.stanford.edu/entries/grotius/ (last visited Apr 7, 2022).

[406] Editors of Encyclopedia Britannica, Alberico Gentili Encyclopedia Britannica (2022), https://www.britannica.com/biography/Alberico-Gentili (last visited Apr 6, 2022).

[407] Hugo Grotius, *in* Law of War and Peace 28 (George Grafton Wilson tran., 1941), https://www.jstor.org/stable/2192260 (last visited Apr 7, 2022).

to write upon the subject. Throughout the Christian world I observed a lack of restraint in relation to war, such as even barbarous races should be ashamed of; I observed that men rush to arms for slight causes, or no cause at all, and that when arms have once been taken up there is no longer any respect for law, divine or human; it is as if, in accordance with a general decree, frenzy had openly been let loose for the committing of all crimes.

Grotius has now acknowledged something that has not yet been examined, the very concept that *international* law is based upon, which is that countries are to each other what people are to each other are from a civil law perspective. All throughout history, there had been a failure to recognize that most fundamental precept; it was constantly danced around, grazed and implied, but never as yet was there explicit recognition of a true *community* of nations that are bound under one common law. Grotius similarly expanded upon Victoria's writings on the neutrality of the seas, emphasizing their access to all[408]. Grotius' work was later seized upon by those that went on to found international organizations, and the concepts he outlined became the rationale for the legality of those organizations.

After Grotius, developments in the field of international law became few and far between until the First Geneva Convention.[409] This was one of the first wide-reaching binding agreements that codified the equitable treatment of combatants in war. Initially, only twelve nations

[408] Hugo Grotius, Mare LIBERUM Wikimedia Commons (RALPH VAN DEMAN MAGOFFIN tran., 1916), https://upload.wikimedia.org/wikipedia/commons/7/7b/Grotius_Hugo_The_Freedom_of_the_Sea_(v1.0).pdf (last visited Apr 7, 2022).
[409] First Geneva Convention for the Amelioration of the Condition of the Wounded in Armies in the Field, *adopted* 1882.

signed the compact, due to the constraints of the intersection of diplomacy and technology. These nations were all Western European. The Convention came about as a result of the efforts of a recently established aid organization, the International Red Cross[410]. The Red Cross, which was created by Swiss entrepreneur Henri Dunant[411], was established as a direct result of Dunant's observations during the Second Italian War of Independence[412] of wanton brutality toward soldiers who were wounded and unable to fight. Dunant had traveled through Lombardy, a region in Northern Italy enroute to France to meet with Napoléon III[413] to discuss trade barriers in North Africa. He passed through the town of Solferino, which had experienced a battle, and he was shocked at what he witnessed - wounded soldiers abandoned upon the battlefield, left to die and rot. However, the soldiers that had been retrieved were subject to similarly horrifying conditions, lacking at an institutional level even barely sufficient medical care. Dunant forsook his original journey, and wrote an account of what he witnessed, entitled *A Memory of*

---

[410] Editors of Encyclopedia Britannica, International Red Cross Encyclopedia Britannica (2018),
https://www.britannica.com/topic/International-Committee-of-the-Red-Cross (last visited Apr 9, 2022).

[411] Editors of Encyclopedia Britannica, Henri Dunant Encyclopedia Britannica (2021),
https://www.britannica.com/topic/International-Committee-of-the-Red-Cross (last visited Apr 9, 2022).

[412] Editors of Encyclopedia Britannica, Wars on Italian Independence Encyclopedia Britannica (2021),
https://www.britannica.com/event/Wars-of-Italian-Independence (last visited Apr 9, 2022).

[413] Heinrich Gustav Euler, Napoleon III Encyclopedia Britannica (2022),
https://www.britannica.com/biography/Napoleon-III-emperor-of-France (last visited Apr 9, 2022).

Solferino[414]. Dunant wrote, in favor of this new international organization -

> On certain special occasions, as, for example, when princes of the military art belonging to different nationalities meet at Cologne or Châlons, would it not be desirable that they should take advantage of this sort of congress to formulate some international principle, sanctioned by a Convention inviolate in character, which, once agreed upon and ratified, might constitute the basis for societies for the relief of the wounded in the different European countries.

The Red Cross grew from there, and expanded into a respected organization consulted frequently by the government of Switzerland. In line with what he wrote, in the early 1860s, Dunant formed a committee of advisors, which worked closely with the Swiss government to develop a tract of proposals, to be presented at a convention in Geneva, and with governmental assent, sent out the invitations, and thus the Geneva Convention of 1864 was born. The Convention empowered the Red Cross to be a truly impartial monitoring institution, responsible for reporting on the adherents of the signatories of the Conventions.

---

[414] Jean-Henry Dunant, A Memory of Solferino International Committee of the Red Cross (2009), https://www.icrc.org/en/doc/assets/files/publications/icrc-002-0361.pdf (last visited Apr 9, 2022).

The Hague Conventions[415] [416] [417] of the late nineteenth and early twentieth centuries built off of the success of the Geneva Convention in a revolutionary way. These conventions, ratified in the wake of Great Power wars of the nineteenth century, served to form the basis of the second, and most substantial to date, wave of multipolar *legal* structures between world powers. Throughout history, there had been treaties, even treaties with numerous parties, such as the Geneva Conventions, but these were almost universally non-enforceable, or concerned purely with *awards*[418] or in modern parlance, "damages," denoting resource transfers, being most often foisted upon the losing party in a conflict. The Hague Conventions, the first of which was organized for Tsar Nicholas II's[419] birthday, specifically codified what the laws of war were, building on the long tradition of Entemena, Confucius, Vyasa, Aristotle, Zeno, Gaius, Cicero, Ulpian, Hermogenianus, Augustine, Aquinas, Vitoria, Gentili, and Grotius. These new international agreements were the most binding to date, and the furthest-ranging to define what the treatment of prisoners

---

[415] Editors of Encyclopedia Britannica, Hague Convention Encyclopedia Britannica (2021),
https://www.britannica.com/event/Hague-Conventions (last visited Apr 6, 2022).

[416] Hague Convention of 1899, *in* The Avalon Project (2008),
https://avalon.law.yale.edu/19th_century/hague01.asp (last visited Apr 7, 2022).

[417] Hague Convention of 1907, *in* The Avalon Project (2008),
https://avalon.law.yale.edu/19th_century/hague01.asp (last visited Apr 7, 2022).

[418] Office of Legal Affairs, United Nations 1-33 Reports of International Arbitral Awards. Recueil des Sentences Arbitrales Codification Publications (1948-2020), https://legal.un.org/riaa/ (last visited Apr 7, 2022).

[419] John L.H. Keep, Nicholas II Encyclopedia Britannica (2021),
https://www.britannica.com/biography/Nicholas-II-tsar-of-Russia (last visited Apr 6, 2022).

was to be, behavior during states of martial law[420], promulgate the creation of an international arbitration court, establish a regulation on the kinds of weapons to be used during war[421] [422] [423], and create a comprehensive list of war crimes. The first ever truly international arbitral forum was created in the form of the Permanent Court of Arbitration[424]. These conventions were based primarily off of an older attempt at the same, the unsuccessful Brussels Declaration of 1874[425], which fell short in the absence of international agreement on the provisions. That declaration was in turn based upon the issuance by U.S. President Abraham Lincoln[426] of the

---

[420] Convention with Respect to the Laws and Customs of War on Land, *in* The Avalon Project (2008),
https://avalon.law.yale.edu/19th_century/hague02.asp (last visited Apr 9, 2022).

[421] Declaration On The Launching Of Projectiles And Explosives From Balloons, *in* The Avalon Project (2008),
https://avalon.law.yale.edu/19th_century/dec99-01.asp (last visited Apr 9, 2022).

[422] Declaration On The Use Of Projectiles The Object Of Which Is The Diffusion Of Asphyxiating Or Deleterious Gasses, *in* The Avalon Project (2008),
https://avalon.law.yale.edu/19th_century/dec99-02.asp (last visited Apr 9, 2022).

[423] Declaration on the Use of Bullets Which Expand or Flatten Easily in the Human Body, *in* The Avalon Project (2008),
https://avalon.law.yale.edu/19th_century/dec99-03.asp (last visited Apr 9, 2022).

[424] Convention For The Pacific Settlement Of International Disputes, *in* The Avalon Project (2008),
https://avalon.law.yale.edu/20th_century/pacific.asp (last visited Apr 9, 2022).

[425] Brussels Declaration of 1874, *opened for signature* July 27th, 1874

[426] Richard N. Current, Abraham Lincoln Encyclopedia Britannica (2022), https://www.britannica.com/biography/Abraham-Lincoln (last visited Apr 6, 2022).

Lieber Code[427] during the American Civil War[428], which was a domestic military order designed to preserve the rule of law during a contentious war.

These Conventions, in the aftermath of World War One[429], provided for a framework for the Entente to arbitrate the total cost of any and all offensive actions by the Central Powers thought to be without cause or alternatively, war crimes. This adjudication became known as the Treaty of Versailles[430], which formally ended the war, set up arbitrators, and ordered reparations. The Treaty included a section[431] establishing the League of Nations[432], the world's first international governmental body. The United States, concerned about possible infringements of national sovereignty, never ratified the Treaty, and was forced to end hostilities separately with the Central Powers via an Act of Congress,[433] The Knox-Porter Resolution. The League of Nations was weakened however, by the relative non-binding nature of its resolutions and compacts. Rulings by the League of Nations had no authority to

---

[427] [War Department], [Gen. Order No. 100] (04/23/1863) [hereinafter Gen. Order No. 100]

[428] Jennifer L. Weber, American Civil War Encyclopedia Britannica (2022), https://www.britannica.com/event/American-Civil-WarI (last visited Apr 6, 2022).

[429] John Graham Royde-Smith, World War 1 Encyclopedia Britannica (2022), https://www.britannica.com/event/World-War-I (last visited Apr 6, 2022).

[430] Treaty of Versailles, *opened for signature* June 28th, 1919

[431] Treaty of Versailles (Covenant of the League of Nations) Pt1., *opened for signature* June 28th, 1919, *id.*

[432] The Editors of Encyclopedia Britannica, League of Nations Encyclopedia Britannica (2020), https://www.britannica.com/topic/League-of-Nations (last visited Apr 7, 2022).

[433] Knox-Porter Resolution, S.J. Res 16, 67th Cong. § 1 (1921).

contravene the sovereign domestic authority of any of its constituent states, and this effectively resulted in a large number of unheeded, exceedingly well written complaints. The League was however responsible for one major arms reduction treaty, the Washington Naval Treaty[434], which sought to reduce the total maximum tonnage of Great Power Navies, so as to prevent a destructive and economically imprudent arms race. In its nadir, around the 1930's, the League sought to litigate acts that it saw as overtly imperialistic, such as the Mukden Incident,[435] an false flag operation utilized by the Empire of Japan to seize Manchuria, the Italian conquest of Abyssinia[436], now called Ethiopia, and the Soviet invasion of Finland.[437] As time went on, and conflicts escalated in severity and scale, the League found itself becoming more and more ineffectual, as rogue governments refused to heed its counsel.

The idea for a power-imbued multinational governmental body came soon after. In 1939, World War Two exploded in Europe when Nazi Germany utilized a similar false flag incident to the Mukden Incident, the

---

[434] Washington Naval Treaty, *adopted* Apr. 16, 1924, 610 L.N.T.S. 609.

[435] League of Nations, Lytton Commission, *Lytton Report*, (02 October 1932), https://www.loc.gov/item/2021666890 (last visited Apr 7, 2022)

[436] George W. Baer, *Ethiopia is Italian - The End of Sanctions*, *in* Test Case: Italy, Ethiopia, and the League of Nations 290 (1976), https://books.google.com/books?id=2bI2tmDPgA0C&printsec=front cover&source=gbs_ge_summary_r&cad=0#v=onepage&q=League& f=false (last visited Apr 7, 2022).

[437] League of Nations, Journal of the League of Nations 20. p509, L.N. C.370.M.283.1939.VII (Dec. 03, 1939), https://heinonline-org.proxyau.wrlc.org/HOL/Page?handle=hein.jour nals/leagon20&id=543&collection=fijournals&index=journals/leago n (last visited Apr 7, 2022)

Gleiwitz Incident[438], to create a pretext for invading the sovereign nation of Poland. The incident in question involved Abwehr and SS staging an attack by "Polish" forces on a radio transmitter in Germany. As the war developed, the League found itself powerless to intervene. Eventually, operations wound down until the League was a shadow of itself, which reduced it to essentially the Secretary-General and his immediate staff. Years passed before the United Nations (the term formally self-ascribed to the Allied Powers and not the international organization of today) realized that there was a need to establish a legal post-war international structure that lacked the weakness of the League in the event of their victory. At the Tehran Conference of 1943[439], President Franklin D. Roosevelt[440] communicated to General Secretary Joseph Stalin[441] his vision for "[the] creation of a "general international organization" designed to promote "international peace and security."" This organization he said, would be meant to be "dominated by "four policemen" (the United States, Britain, China, and Soviet Union) who "would have the power to deal immediately with any threat to

---

[438] Case Against the S.S., 4 Avalon Project 24 (1945), https://avalon.law.yale.edu/subject_menus/imtproc_v4menu.asp (last visited Apr 7, 2022).

[439] Historian, Department of State, Tehran Conference of 1943 U.S. Department of State, https://history.state.gov/milestones/1937-1945/tehran-conf (last visited Apr 7, 2022).

[440] Frank Freidel, Franklin Delano Roosevelt Encyclopedia Britannica (2022), https://www.britannica.com/biography/Franklin-D-Roosevelt (last visited Apr 6, 2022).

[441] Ronald Francis Hingley, Franklin Delano Roosevelt Encyclopedia Britannica (2022), https://www.britannica.com/biography/Joseph-Stalin (last visited Apr 6, 2022).

the peace and any sudden emergency which requires action.""""

Indeed, when World War Two had concluded, with the surrender of Nazi Germany at Flensburg on May 6th, 1945, and Imperial Japan on September 2nd of the same year aboard the USS Missouri in the wake of the atomic bombings of Hiroshima and Nagasaki, the Allies were free to pursue their goal of an international governmental body endowed with real power. In San Francisco, after the surrender of Germany, but before the surrender of Japan, the nations of the world gathered at the Veterans Building to sign the founding Charter on June 26th, and the Charter went into effect in October, after a total cessation of hostilities in both Europe and Asia. The Charter was revolutionary because its explicit purpose, and that of the nascent United Nations, as outlined in the first declarative line[442] of the preamble, was to "to save succeeding generations from the scourge of war, which twice in our lifetime has brought untold sorrow to mankind." This was the first instance in human history where a plurinational organization had chiefly dedicated itself to the preservation of peace without avarice. Previously, peace agreements, even multipolar ones, had generally sought to prevent war for the sake of economic stability, or strategic aim. The Charter further elaborates that the duty of all nations assembled is to not only preserve peace but to "to reaffirm faith in fundamental human rights, in the dignity and worth of the human person, in the equal rights of men and women and of nations large and small, and to establish conditions under which justice and respect for the obligations arising from treaties and other sources of international law can be

---

[442]United Nations Charter Preamble, United Nations Conference on International Organization, para.1. (1945)

maintained, and to promote social progress and better standards of life in larger freedom." The Allies additionally conducted extensive trials at Tokyo and Nuremberg, attempting to codify into international precedent the concept of a "crime against humanity." The judges, who were appointed by the sovereign leaders of each nation on the Allied side, elected to effectively create new crimes in addition to prosecuting old ones, such as crimes against humanity, and waging wars of aggression. In writing this new jurisprudence, the judges relied both upon philosophy, and previous international treaties.

Famed poet Alfred Lord Tennyson, writing of his vision of the future in his *Locksley Hall*[443] once wrote -

> For I dipt into the future, far as human eye could see, Saw the Vision of the world, and all the wonder that would be; Saw the heavens fill with commerce, argosies of magic sails, Pilots of the purple twilight dropping down with costly bales; Heard the heavens fill with shouting, and there rain'd a ghastly dew From the nations' airy navies grappling in the central blue; Far along the world-wide whisper of the south-wind rushing warm, With the standards of the peoples plunging thro' the thunder-storm; Till the war-drum throbbed no longer, and the battle-flags were fool'd, In the Parliament of man, the Federation of the world. There the common sense of most shall hold a fretful realm in awe, And the kindly earth shall slumber, lapt in *universal law*.

Tennyson may have not been a scholar of technology or international law, but he foresaw a world dominated by

---

[443] Alfred Tennyson Tennyson & W. D. Ticknor, *Locksley Hall, 119-130, in* Poems (1842).

technology, specifically in the fields of aviation, munitions and commerce, as well as a defined international body that worked to prevent war. During World War Two, the need for adaptation to rapidly advancing technology was painfully apparent, as strategies such as strategic bombing and automatic weapons usage became prevalent. There is no incident more fitting for this rationale than the atomic bombings of Japan, which demonstrated humanity's ability to wage war in a fashion that could very well prove apocalyptic. In keeping with Tennyson's vision, the body of international law grew quickly to fit rapidly developing technology. In the Cold War years, the United Nations used its newfound legal power to arbitrate conflicts, and to attempt to prevent them, something the organization proved far more effective at than its predecessor. The International Court of Justice[444] was established, following the ideals of its counterpart in the League of Nations, providing for a new forum for global arbitration. As time passed, new organs grew to fill the needs of these United Nations, not just on military affairs, but also on matters of environmental law[445], maritime law[446], aviation law[447], copyright law[448], and

---

[444] United Nations Charter XIV, United Nations Conference on International Organization (1945)

[445] UN Environment Program, About UN Environment Programme UNEP, https://www.unep.org/about-un-environment (last visited Apr 7, 2022).

[446] Brief history of the IMO, IMO | History of IMO (2015), https://web.archive.org/web/20150511184000/http://www.imo.org/About/HistoryOfIMO/Pages/Default.aspx (last visited Apr 7, 2022).

[447] About ICAO, ICAO, https://www.icao.int/about-icao/Pages/default.aspx (last visited Apr 7, 2022).

[448] Convention Establishing The World Intellectual Property Organization, *adopted* July 14th, 1967, U.N.T.S. 2186 (p.121).

fundamentally, human rights law[449]. To this day, the U.N. serves, through these organs as the final court of plea for those seeking to obtain judgment internationally, whether that be militarily in the form of peacekeeping operations[450], judicially in the form of ICJ rulings, or economically in the form of the International Monetary Fund[451], all serving the community of the United Nations.

All throughout the ages, philosophers, and even statesmen, had gone back and forth debating, on the merits of natural law, and the delineation of entities to be considered sovereign, and the rights of the people in all of it, but never had such a wide ranging group of countries banded together to say with one voice, that there are indeed unalienable rights and that justice, not strength should be the primary aim of conflict. Those sentiments, that were laid down at the feet of sovereigns stretching back to Mesopotamia, by Aristotle and Cicero, by Augustine and Aquinas, by Vitoria and Vyasa, and by myriad others, were finally recognized to be legal doctrine. And thus, the definition of entity that Entemena made, followed by the recognition by Aristotle and Zeno of natural law, then the delineations that Cicero, Gaius, Ulpian, and Hermogenianus drew between domestic law, natural law, and national law all became material, and

---

[449] Welcome to the Human Rights Council, UN Human Rights Council, https://www.ohchr.org/en/hr-bodies/hrc/about-council (last visited Apr 7, 2022).

[450] Department of Peace Operations Peacekeeping, United Nations Department of Peace Operations, https://peacekeeping.un.org/en/department-of-peace-operations (last visited Apr 7, 2022).

[451] The IMF at a Glance, IMF (2019), https://www.imf.org/en/About/Factsheets/IMF-at-a-Glance (last visited Apr 7, 2022).

the field of international law was truly born as Vitoria and Aquinas hoped, equally and justly towards both sovereign and people, between a true community of United Nations as envisaged by Grotius.

DEFINING *CASUS BELLI* AND *CASUS FOEDERIS*

Casus belli and casus foederis together form two of the three legally justifiable defenses for the initiation of a conflict. Casus belli is broadly defined as the legal cause for war, while casus foederis is broadly defined as the joining in of a conflict as a result of a treaty or compact held between two or more nations. In that sense, casus foederis can be considered both a discrete justification for war and a subset of casus belli. These terms are unique, because they constitute instances in which a state, or states can unilaterally, without the predecisional assent of the United Nations, initiate a conflict. This right, both in terms of a response to an attack on a sovereign nation, or its allies, is outlined in terms of international law most expressly in Article 51[452] of the Charter of the U.N., wherein it states -

> Nothing in the present Charter shall impair the inherent right of individual or collective self-defense if an armed attack occurs against a Member of the United Nations, until the Security Council has taken measures necessary to maintain international peace and security. Measures taken by Members in the exercise of this right of self-defense shall be immediately reported to the Security Council and shall not in any way affect the authority and responsibility of the Security Council under the present Charter to take at any time such action as it

---

[452] United Nations Charter LI, United Nations Conference on International Organization (1945)

deems necessary in order to maintain or restore international peace and security.

It is important to recognize that whilst the United Nations does outline that casus belli is met when self-defense is invoked, the Charter is unclear on what qualifications are required to meet the term "armed attack." Additionally, as noted, the Charter requires an immediate notification to the United Nations Security Council that casus belli is being invoked for their consideration and adjudication. The United Nations Security Council[453] is one of the six "principal organs" of the United Nations, responsible for establishing and maintaining peacekeeping forces[454], compelling arbitration,[455] implementing sanctions[456], and along with the General Assembly in certain cases, approving military action by member states, or as a collective body[457]. This requirement to notify does not prevent any nation from taking offensive action if it, or an ally, legitimately *feels* threatened, but at any time the Security Council is empowered to litigate the justification. Historically, the U.N. Security Council has responded to acts of aggression that it feels are unwarranted, even when the belligerent believes that it is in the right. A prime example of this, and one where the collective security mission of the Security Council succeeded in

---

[453] United Nations Charter VII, United Nations Conference on International Organization (1945)

[454] United Nations Charter XLIII, United Nations Conference on International Organization (1945)

[455] United Nations Charter XXXIII-XXXVIII, United Nations Conference on International Organization (1945)

[456] United Nations Charter XLI, United Nations Conference on International Organization (1945)

[457] United Nations Charter XLII, United Nations Conference on International Organization (1945)

constructive implementation, was the creation of United Nations Command,[458] [459] [460] in response to the Sino-Soviet backed North Korean invasion of the South in 1950[461]. The Security Council considered the matter upon petition, and concluded that intervention was necessary to both prevent undue loss of life and contain the hostilities to the Korean peninsula. In this qualification under the Charter, casus belli is defined as a significantly more subjective concept, being dependent upon the attitudes of command authorities who interpret events directed at states of which they are executives of. Casus foederis on the other hand, relates to an incident in which the terms of a bilateral or multilateral treaty compel a nation to come to the defense of an ally which has been attacked. The ally in question would have achieved Casus belli primarily, but the party bound by the treaty would invoke Casus foederis. The definition of Casus foederis is far more codified, and could be considered effectively *performance*[462] of a contract, not a subjective assessment of an event. Typically, when Casus foederis is invoked, it is at the request of the ally, which constitutes, almost universally, a notification clause within the treaty. Thus, the definition of Casus belli is far more open to interpretation in original action than Casus foederis. In line with that, historically, the

---

[458] U.N.S.C.. Res. 82, U.N. SCOR, 5th Sess, U.N.Doc. S/1501, (Jun. 25th, 1950)

[459] U.N.S.C.. Res. 83, U.N. SCOR, 5th Sess, U.N.Doc. S/1511, (Jun. 27th, 1950)

[460] U.N.S.C.. Res. 84, U.N. SCOR, 5th Sess, U.N.Doc. S/1588, (Jul. 7th, 1950)

[461] Allan R. Millett, Korean War Encyclopedia Britannica (2021), https://www.britannica.com/event/Korean-War(last visited Apr 8, 2022).

[462] Wex Definitions Team, Performance Wex (2020), https://www.law.cornell.edu/wex/performance (last visited Apr 10, 2022).

United Nations has by force of its Charter, interpreted Casus belli on a case by case basis.

INCLUSION AND EXCLUSION UNDER
THE CHARTER OF THE UNITED NATIONS

American novelist Truman Capote[463] once said "The problem with living outside the law is that you no longer have its protection." The Charter specifies that in order for an attack to be considered as such, it must be directed at a nation currently a member of the United Nations, wherein it explicitly employs that phrase, specifying - "if an armed attack occurs against a Member of the United Nations."[464] Under a plain-text reading of the clause, a nation such as the Republic of China, which was expelled from the body by U.N. General Assembly Resolution 2758[465] in favor of granting the country's seat to the People's Republic of China, would be effectively open to attack without consequences, and conversely, would not be able to have its potential belligerency considered against any nation that was a member of the United Nations. Ten years before Resolution 2758 was

---

[463] Kathleen Kuiper, Truman Capote Encyclopedia Britannica (2021), https://www.britannica.com/biography/Truman-Capote (last visited Apr 19, 2022).

[464] United Nations Charter LI, United Nations Conference on International Organization (1945) *supra* 91

[465] U.N.G.A.. Res. 2758, U.N. GAOR, 26th Sess, U.N.Doc. A/RES/2758(XXVI), (Oct. 25th, 1971)

promulgated, the Prime Minister of Nepal, B.P. Koirala[466] suggested[467] to the UN General Assembly that:

> In our [sic] opinion, the United Nations can neither become universal nor can it reflect the political realities existing in the world today until the People's Republic of China is given its rightful place in the organization. The United Nations will not be able to fulfill effectively some of its most important purposes and functions until the People's Republic of China is brought in.

B.P. Koirala, a noted champion of democracy, and one of Nepal's early democratically elected prime ministers had rightfully reasoned that the exclusion of millions of people from the United Nations, a body that in its founding charter expresses the intent to represent all of the peoples of the world[468]. However, the solution that was enacted, the revocation and reallocation of representation from the Republic of China to the People's Republic of China constitutes perhaps a net enfranchisement numerically, but disbars millions of people from being considered as constituents of a discrete sovereign entity. Under international law as interpreted by the U.N., neither casus belli nor casus foederis must be presented nor even expressed should a member state feel it necessary to engage in military action against a non-member entity. Many such

---

[466] Reuters, *B.P. Koirala, Former Prime Minister of Nepal*, New York Times, July 22, 1982, at 19, https://www.nytimes.com/1982/07/22/obituaries/bp-koirala-former-prime-minister-of-nepal.html (last visited Apr 9, 2022).

[467] B.P. Koirala, Address by Prime Minister B.P. Koirala of Nepal on the Matter of the China Question United Nations General Assembly (1960).

[468] United Nations Charter Preamble, United Nations Conference on International Organization, para.1. *supra* (1945)

non-member entities currently exist, including the Republic of China, the State of Palestine, the Sahrawi Arab Democratic Republic, the Turkish Republic of Northern Cyprus, the Republic of South Ossetia, the Republic of Abkhazia, the Pridnestrovian Moldavian Republic, the Republic of Artsakh, and the Republic of Somaliland. In addition, there exists, in the regions of the world not yet touched by modern civilization, communities of people living "uncontacted." The sum total of peoples living under this designation is in the millions, and represents merely individuals that have not recognizably to the U.N. declared themselves to comprise larger political entities, i.e. by declaring independence, a principle known as the "declarative theory"[469] under the Montevideo Convention of 1933, which was originally a limited treaty amongst American nations, but has since, through reverse incorporation, become an established facet of international law. However, the requirements insofar as casus belli and casus foederis legally do not reflect this, and consider effectively those populations to be unprotected under the Charter's "self-defense" clause. This has created an unequal dynamic in which millions of people are legally open to attack under the founding Charter.

OTHER FORMS OF ENSHRINED REQUIREMENTS TO JUSTIFY WAR

Whilst the United Nations Charter and subsidiary laws are one, perhaps dominating, form of international law, there exists other multilateral frameworks for the regulation of war. One notable example is the

---

[469] Montevideo Convention on the Rights and Duties of States *adopted* Dec. 26th, 1933, U.N.T.S. 3802 165 (p.19).

Kellogg-Briand Pact[470], named for U.S. Secretary of State Frank B. Kellogg[471] and French Foreign Minister Aristide Briand[472], created in parallel with the Geneva Convention for the Pacific Settlement of International Disputes[473], was meant to preferentially enshrine pacifism in the foreign policy of the world's great powers. The Kellogg-Briand Pact was quite simplistic, and formulaically only contained two one-sentence provisions, wherein it states -

> A) The High Contracting Parties solemnly declare in the names of their respective peoples that they condemn recourse to war for the solution of international controversies and renounce it as an instrument of national policy in their relations with one another. B) The High Contracting Parties agree that the settlement or solution of all disputes or conflicts of whatever nature or of whatever origin they may be, which may arise among them, shall never be sought except by pacific means.

Although perhaps needlessly simplistic and reductive, and somewhat devoid of recourse, the Pact was utilized by the judges at both the Nuremberg Trials and the Tokyo War Crimes Tribunal. Nazi Germany and the Empire of Japan were signatories to the Pact, and

---

[470] General Treaty for Renunciation of War as an Instrument of National Policy *adopted* Aug. 27th, 1928, L.N.T.S. 2137 94 (p.57).
[471] The Editors of Encyclopedia Britannica, Frank B. Kellogg Encyclopedia Britannica (2021), https://www.britannica.com/biography/Frank-B-Kellogg (last visited Apr 12, 2022).
[472] The Editors of Encyclopedia Britannica, Aristide Briand Encyclopedia Britannica (2022), https://www.britannica.com/biography/Aristide-Briand (last visited Apr 12, 2022).
[473] General Act for the Pacific Settlement of International Disputes *adopted* Aug. 16th, 1929, L.N.T.S. 2123 93 (p.343).

therefore, the argument was made, and which has consistently held up under scrutiny, that a violation of this Pact for the single purpose of aggrandizing one's or one's ally's territory, is in fact a violation of international law. The Allied Occupation Authorities utilized the trials to execute and imprison offenders perceived to be in violation of this Pact. Even perhaps if the text of the Pact was a tad vague, the sentiments of preferential pacific foreign policy contained within are not only ironclad, but are still in effect today, and the crime of *waging a war of aggression* is and has been enshrined in international law. This has been parallelly codified in the United Nations Charter, under Article II, Section IV, wherein it states - "All Members shall refrain in their international relations from the threat or use of force against the territorial integrity or political independence of any state, or in any other manner inconsistent with the Purposes of the United Nations."[474] However, something important to note is that enforcement of the U.N. Charter requires the initiative and assent of the United Nations, which is a high level of qualified agreement that one has to reach to take action. Conversely, the Kellogg-Briand Pact, which at one point had as a recording body, not an enforcing body, in the League of Nations, no longer has such an international body, leaving the enforcement of the Pact up to signatory nations, as is what occurred during the postwar war crimes tribunals.

Another important distinct piece of international law, disconnected in theory from the U.N., which speaks of casus belli and presents an enforceable compact for signatories is the Rome Statute of the International

---

[474] United Nations Charter II, United Nations Conference on International Organization (1945)

Criminal Court[475]. The Rome Statute effectively bridges the gaps in both specificity and enforcement that were present in the Kellogg-Briand Pact, and created an international enforcing body, the International Criminal Court[476], headquartered in The Hague, in the Netherlands. The Rome Statute created original[477] and "parallel"[478] jurisdiction (although based on the definition of these terms, this is disputable) for the court over four types of war crimes, and their subsets, building on the sentiments of the Kellogg-Briand Pact, and codifying them into enforceable law. These four basic types of crimes are: genocide, crimes against humanity, crimes committed during the prosecution of war, and waging wars of aggression[479]. The Rome Statute outlines these -

> The jurisdiction of the Court shall be limited to the most serious crimes of concern to the international community as a whole. The Court has jurisdiction in accordance with this Statute with respect to the following crimes: (a) The crime of genocide; (b) Crimes against humanity; (c) War crimes; (d) The crime of aggression.

---

[475] The Statute of the International Criminal Court *opened for signature in July.* 17th, 1998, U.N.T.S. 38544 2187 (p.3).

[476] About the Court, ICC , https://www.icc-cpi.int/about/the-court (last visited Apr 18, 2022).

[477] Original jurisdiction, Wex Legal Encyclopedia (1992), https://www.law.cornell.edu/wex/original_jurisdiction (last visited Apr 18, 2022).

[478] Dictionary Definitions, Parallel Jurisdiction Free Online Dictionary of Law Terms and Legal Definitions (2020), https://legaldictionary.lawin.org/parallel-jurisdiction/#:~:text=Meaning%20of%20Parallel%20Jurisdiction%20The%20term%20derives%20its,issues%20necessary%20to%20resolution%20of%20a%20Federal%20claim. (last visited Apr 18, 2022).

[479] Rome Statute of the International Criminal Court Art. 5-8, p.2-9 *opened for signature in July.* 17th, 1998, U.N.T.S. 38544 2187 (p.3).

The Court is entirely separate from the United Nations, and is not reliant upon it for authority, but rather, is structured in a similar manner, with the Court being reliant upon signatory nations for enforcement. Interestingly, funding for the court is allocated and collected in a manner similar to the United Nations, in proportion to economic power. The Court to date has enforced this clause successfully nine times through in ten convictions[480], one of which was reversed, that of Congolese Vice President Jean-Pierre Bemba.[481] The Court, while not overseen by the U.N., was created by it through the negotiation of the Rome Statute, and allows the U.N. Security Council to either refer cases to the Court, or conversely, prevent the Court from proceeding against a defendant.[482] However, these convictions, while notable steps in international law, are at the mercy of signatory nations to elect to enforce the decisions. If signatory nations disagree, then the Court is powerless to enforce the decisions it renders.

One might think that the Court is similar to the U.N. in this respect, but the U.N, whilst retaining a similar structure of authority, has as member states almost every nation in existence, most importantly the five great

---

[480] About the Court, ICC , https://www.icc-cpi.int/about/the-court (last visited Apr 18, 2022) *supra* 115.

[481] The Prosecutor v. Jean-Pierre Bemba Gombo, Aimé Kilolo Musamba, Jean-Jacques Mangenda Kabongo, Fidèle Babala Wandu and Narcisse Arido, No. ICC-01/05-01/13 A A2 A3 A4 A5 ICC (2018), https://www.icc-cpi.int/sites/default/files/CourtRecords/CR2018_016 38.PDF (last visited Apr 18, 2022).

[482] Rome Statute of the International Criminal Court Art. 13,16,53, 57,87,115 p.10-60 *opened for signature in July.* 17th, 1998, U.N.T.S. 38544 2187 (p.3).

powers of the United States, the Russian Federation, the United Kingdom, the People's Republic of China, and the Republic of France. Of those selected nations, which are the states with the most power to enforce international law decisions, three do not belong to the Court, and have not signed the Rome Statute. Russia, China, and the United States, collectively representing a population of 1.9 billion people, all of whom are not subject to the Court's authority. This is roughly equivalent to a fourth of all humans on Earth. Opposition to the Court's authority most often comes in these nations in the form of a perceived loss of sovereignty. For example, though President Bill Clinton[483] signed the Rome Statute in 2000, opposition to the Court's perceived encroachment on domestic law in the United States was so great, that in 2002, the U.S. Congress passed the American Service-Member Protection Act (ASPA),[484] which prohibits the U.S. government from cooperating with the Court, prevents the transfer of military aid to Rome Statute signatories (with strategic exceptions), and compels the United States to rescue American service members being tried by the Court. The Act goes so far as to state that it "...Authorizes the President to use all means necessary (including the provision of legal assistance) to bring about the release of covered U.S. persons and covered allied persons held captive by, on behalf, or at the request of the Court."[485] This clause quite literally enables the government to invade the Netherlands to recover any American service

---

[483] The Editors of Encyclopedia Britannica, BIll Clinton
Encyclopedia Britannica (2021),
https://www.britannica.com/biography/Bill-Clinton (last visited Apr 19, 2022).
[484] American Service-Members Protection Act, H.R. 4775, 107th Cong. § 2 (2002).
[485] *id.*

member being tried before the Court. Historically, the United States has been open to the idea of the establishment of an international court, but has interpreted the implementation as an infringement on domestic sovereignty, choosing to endorse a "rules for thee, but not for me" approach, wherein a case brought before the Court concerning a foreign national of a neutral or enemy country would be most likely be lauded, but any case involving a U.S. citizen or NATO[486] ally would not, and would be met with force, whether economic, diplomatic, or military in nature.

Another significant issue that contests the legitimacy of the Court's authority is that of the Court's tendency to singularly investigate and indict alleged offenders whose allegiance lies with less powerful, less prominent, and primarily non-Western nations, with the vast majority of defendants and investigations originating in African countries. Every single ICC defendant to date has been charged in association with service to an African nation, while every investigation has taken place in the Middle East, Africa, or Eastern Europe.[487] This is a direct result of the way that the Court's charter operates, with far more freedom granted to powerful belligerents, and a stricter view taken toward nations of small economic, military, or diplomatic power. This is additionally a result of the fact that the Court does not enforce international law upon non-signatory nations. There have been many equivalent crimes committed by U.S., Russian, and Chinese soldiers, and yet the only

---

[486] David G. Haglund, NATO Encyclopedia Britannica (2022), https://www.britannica.com/topic/North-Atlantic-Treaty-Organization (last visited Apr 19, 2022).
[487] Defendants: International Criminal Court, Defendants | International Criminal Court (2022), https://www.icc-cpi.int/defendants (last visited Apr 19, 2022).

individuals that the Court takes the view are prosecutable are those from underdeveloped nations. This is in contrast to the United Nations, where a nation need not be a member for the body to take action against it. Finally, the Court's hands are tied due to the fact that through the Rome Statute, the U.N. Security Council is empowered to overrule any decision made,[488] and those nations that control the Security Council, the 5 great powers, have not, and most likely would not, agree to comply unless threatened with force. However, it is worth noting that, under a unique set of circumstances in which the Security Council refers a case for persecution to the Court, the U.N., not the Court, may compel the participation of U.N. member states, wherein it states - "The Members of the United Nations agree to accept and carry out the decisions of the Security Council in accordance with the present Charter."[489] Barring this, no state which is not a signatory to the Rome Statute has any obligation to accede to the decisions of the Court. This creates a massive gap between ideals and enforcement, and creates a very real problem for those seeking to prevent and prosecute those who wage wars of aggression or commit crimes against humanity, war crimes, or genocide.

CASUS FOEDERIS AND ITS PLACE WITHIN CASUS BELLI

Casus belli is a well known term, one discussed at length within this article. However, casus foederis, its lesser

---

[488] Rome Statute of the International Criminal Court Art. 16 p.13 *opened for signature in July.* 17th, 1998, U.N.T.S. 38544 2187 (p.3). *Supra* 121.

[489] United Nations Charter XXV, United Nations Conference on International Organization (1945)

known fellow, is equally important in determining whether a war is legal and just. Casus foederis is widely accepted to be one of the three legal justifications under international law for going to war, being the fulfillment of a mutual treaty of common defense. Casus belli, comprises the justificable cause of war, and therefore, the fulfillment of such a treaty, recognized as a legitimate form of recourse, would be considered a justifiable cause. Therefore, it should be recognized that casus belli represents both a term for the whole body of justifications that one is entitled to declare war under, and parallelly, a subset of the same, representing harm to an individual state (original casus belli). However, this distinction is not made particularly clear within international law. Indeed, it is unknown whether a state can reasonably claim that the invocation of a mutual defense pact constitutes a harm against a nation compelled to join the fight by said treaty. For example, the North Atlantic Treaty Organization (NATO) has within its founding Charter, the oft speculated about Article 5, which states that[490] -

> The Parties agree that an armed attack against one or more of them in Europe or North America shall be considered an attack against them all and consequently they agree that, if such an armed attack occurs, each of them, in exercise of the right of individual or collective self-defense recognised by Article 51 of the Charter of the United Nations, will assist the Party or Parties so attacked by taking forthwith, individually and in concert with the other Parties, such action as it deems necessary, including the use of armed force, to restore and maintain the security of the North Atlantic area.

---

[490] North Atlantic Treaty Art. 5 *adopted* Apr. 4th, 1949.

Within this treaty, an attack perpetrated against one member state of the organization is legally found to constitute an attack upon all, and the invocation of Article 5 may very well constitute the same. As such, the lines between casus belli as it applies to a nation singularly and directly and casus foederis as applied to compacts between nations, are blurred significantly. Furthermore, it is not clear if the compact by which a nation called into war must be evaluated to be in compliance with international law, or even rational. For example, if there are two nations, one of which (A) calls the other (B) into a war due to the fact, that under their hypothetical treaty of mutual defense, if it rains on a particular day, that is considered to be an attack from a third nation (C), then it is clear that nation A does not have casus belli under any recognized form of international law. However, if nation B were to declare war under casus foederis, it is not clear if the treaty invoked must have as a prerequisite, a legal definition of casus belli that must be met, but rather it is implied without statements to the contrary, that it is a perfectly defensible reason to go to war so long as an ally calls a nation into one, no matter the cause, because the primary catalyst for the war was not the offensive action perpetrated against nation A, but rather the invocation of a mutual defense pact. This is the problem of casus foederis, and why it is difficult to define, within or separate from original (meaning directly against a state) casus belli.

FINDING A WIDELY ACCEPTED
VIEW OF CASUS BELLI

Finally, Casus belli is a topic that divides scholars, legal authorities, and nations throughout the world. It is impossible to find one, unifying view of what does and does not constitute a moral rationale for declaring war. However, there are widely accepted legal qualifications that one can surmise encompass the breadth of justifiable causes of war. In order to name these properly, it is important to discuss what is widely held *not* to be a justifiable cause. Firstly, the Kellogg-Briand Pact[491], the Rome Statute of the International Criminal Court[492], and the Charter of the United Nations[493] all recognize that "wars of aggression" are to be considered illegal under international law, the term "aggression" being defined as those wars which are initiated primarily for the sake of aggrandizing a nation's own assets, whether they be land, population, materiel, or any combination of the three in addition to wars intended to aggrandize a nation's reputation or perceived strength. The more complex piece is placing a widely accepted definition of what constitutes a just war outside of a war of aggression, within a war initiated due to a perceived threat. In the most widely accepted sense, the role of the word "perceived" is minimized when an attack has materialized in force, and has been affected already against a target. This essentially means that if an attack has been conducted, one in which material harm has been caused, specifically by a state actor, then a nation may consider casus belli to be fulfilled. However, whilst most, if not all authorities agree on a material attack constituting casus belli, a much more divisive topic is

---

[491] General Treaty for Renunciation of War as an Instrument of National Policy *adopted* Aug. 27th, 1928, L.N.T.S. 2137 94 (p.57). *Supra* 109.

[492] Rome Statute of the International Criminal Court Art. 5 p.3 *opened for signature in July.* 17th, 1998, U.N.T.S. 38544 2187 (p.3). *Supra* 127.

[493] United Nations Charter II, United Nations Conference on International Organization (1945)

whether or not casus belli is met via the anticipation of an attack, in the case of a "preemptive" attack. Preemptive war is a delicate subject within international law, and scholars such as Grotius have stated effectively that for casus belli to be met, one must have evidence of an attack's immanence, not merely an "assumption" of attack. He wrote in *The Law of War and Peace*[494], stating -

> War in defense of life is permissible only when the danger is immediate and certain, not when it is merely assumed. 1. The danger, again, must be immediate and imminent at that point of time. I admit, to be sure, that if the assailant seizes weapons in such a way that his intent to kill is manifest the crime can be forestalled;...Further, if a man is not planning an immediate attack, but it has been ascertained that he has formed a plot, or is preparing an ambuscade, or that he is putting poison in our way, or that he is making ready a false accusation and false evidence, and is corrupting the judicial procedure, I maintain that he cannot lawfully be killed, either if the danger can in any other way be avoided, or if it is not altogether certain that the danger cannot be otherwise avoided.

These sentiments have been echoed in an implied-in-fact sense internationally, but it has long been held to be true by national governments. For example, the Caroline affair of the 1800's, between the United States and Canada, formed the basis for the customs that were enshrined in the Nuremberg Trials and later in the U.N.

---

[494] Hugo Grotius, *in* Law of War and Peace 2 | 5 (George Grafton Wilson tran., 1941), https://www.jstor.org/stable/2192260 (last visited Apr 7, 2022). *supra* 46

Charter. The Caroline affair occurred in 1837, when settlers in Upper Canada rebelled against the British government. Covertly, the United States began supplying the rebels, and when the British learned of this, a force was sent into the United States to burn a supply ship, the Caroline, and prevent war materiel from reaching the rebels. Daniel Webster, the Secretary of State at the time, rebuffed British claims of self-defense, and classified the act as an unprovoked invasion, due to the fact that the British had failed to prove in their claim that -

> ...necessity of self-defense was instant, overwhelming, leaving no choice of means, and no moment of deliberation ..., and that the British force, even supposing the necessity of the moment authorized them to enter the territories of the United States at all, did nothing unreasonable or excessive; since the act, justified by the necessity of self-defense, must be limited by that necessity, and kept clearly within it.[495]

This event, Webster's repudiation of which was accepted by the British government, formed the basis for the criteria for preemptive war, and was directly referenced by jurists at Nuremberg over 100 years later. To date, the Caroline "test" is a strong, yet uncodified principle of casus belli which has been found to be enforceable when discussing wars of aggression. The U.N. Charter notably does not discuss the possibility of a preemptive attack, electing only to authorize offensive action if an "armed attack occurs against a Member of the United

---

[495] Daniel Webster, Extract of a letter from Mr. Webster to Mr. Fox, dated April 24, 1841, Enclosure 1-Extract from note of April 24,1841 Avalon Project (2008), https://avalon.law.yale.edu/19th_century/br-1842d.asp (last visited Apr 21, 2022).

Nations."[496] The word occurs in this instance is taken to mean *already* has occurred, and the offensive action would then be a response. However, there are instances in which the law, being tremendously important, is on occasion eclipsed by the necessity of survival, and the gray area of the Caroline test must be entered to preserve a state imminently under attack. For example, the State of Israel, during Operation Focus[497], which took place at the beginning of the Six-Day War,[498] Israeli Air Force units under the command of Major General Mordechai Hod[499] preemptively attacked the Egyptian Air Force at 11 air bases, effectively destroying the operational air capability of the Egyptians for the duration of the war. This attack took place before a formal declaration of war on either side, or any detectable materially offensive actions, and so was declared to be an instance of preemptive war. However, Egypt asserted that due to the fact that no offensive action had yet been taken on their part, but rather that Egyptian jets were either on the tarmac or in hangars, it could not be considered justifiable, as an attack was not "imminent." This raises an interesting question, one of quantifying how far along into the process of fomenting an attack a nation must be before opening itself up to a "preemptive" attack. It

---

[496] United Nations Charter LI, United Nations Conference on International Organization (1945) *supra* 91.

[497] ISR MOD, Six Day War Israeli Air Force, https://www.iaf.org.il/2557-30101-en/IAF.aspx (last visited Apr 22, 2022).

[498] The Editors of Encyclopedia Britannica, Six Day War Encyclopedia Britannica (2021), https://www.britannica.com/event/Six-Day-War (last visited Apr 21, 2022).

[499] Uri Dromi, *Motti Hod, 77, IAF Commander*, Haaretz, June 30, 2003, https://www.haaretz.com/1.5487740 (last visited Apr 21, 2022).

raises the further question, drawing the previous one to an extreme, of whether or not merely evidence of the intent of an adversary is sufficient to merit a preemptive attack. It is far less recognized that merely intent constitutes casus belli, particularly within a vacuum. However, there is an argument to be made that intent, when coupled with the *capability* to pose a threat to a nation, may necessitate action on the part of the potential target. This argument scales, particularly when considering the speed at which an adversary may elicit a surrender, taking into account factors such as strategic depth, rapid offensive capabilities, and the potential defense a nation could reasonably mount. In scenarios where a nation resembles a "glass cannon," or is in a position where it may possess significant, outsized offensive capabilities, and yet, when attacked, would capitulate disproportionately quickly in the face of an offensively weaker opponent. This creates a space where a nation could reasonably argue that a "first strike" policy is both legal and necessary to preserve a state; the argument being that a potential attack from an adversary would pose such a threat that the survival of the state would be threatened, that a nation must weigh the intent vs. capability matrix, and may elect to preemptively defeat the threat. However, the main issue is not one of contention between legal authorities, or that the authorities cannot settle on one definition, but rather more specifically, that the definition, however fluid, is subject to the decision not of an impartial investigative body, but rather ultimately, the decision of the highly politicized United Nations. This represents not only an issue with defining preemptive war and preventing unjustified assaults, but an issue in enforcing the entire body of law concerning casus belli.

THE VICE OF SUBJECTIVITY

Subjectivity can be considered an asset, especially when appreciation of the unique facts of a case is an important factor. However, when determining whether or not a crime has been committed, and particularly when establishing the facts of a case, *objectivity* is crucial in determining whether or not a breach of the law has occurred. The structures that constitute the enforcement apparatus of the international community are at an initial level unbiased on paper, and value the principle of due process, but at the highest level, are political in nature. The initial ICC investigation or U.N. investigation and finding may indeed respect the rule of law, but as a case grows in importance and moves up the chain of command, the rules and principles of equal justice go out the window in a formal sense. The U.N. Security Council, and General Assembly are political bodies, and as they (most often the Security Council) have oversight of any incident that may occur, and as the nations permanently seated on the Security Council have a veto power,[500] Most serious incidents are resolved not on the basis of justice, but rather on the basis of geopolitical sentiment.

The structure of the veto system means that the solutions that are arrived at are most often the ones that are the least offensive to any of the five permanent members. This leads to constant bickering and debate, especially when there is a difference in opinion on what constitutes casus belli. Unfortunately, when even one permanent member of the Council disagrees, even if a serious crime has occured, or casus belli is met and requires

---

[500] United Nations Charter XVII, United Nations Conference on International Organization (1945).

evaluation, the truth of the matter may not, and often does not, win out. If there is built into the superstructure of not only the United Nations but the International Criminal Court the ability to overrule the truth and prosecute and conversely, deflect investigations by political means, then the definition of casus belli as it stands, no matter how it is legally codified, is *de facto* null and void, effectively a perverse victor's justice. The rule of law is only a significant factor where it is respected, and it is clear that that is, but up until the point where it no longer serves geopolitical concerns. There have been many war crimes and acts of aggression since the United Nations' founding that have not only gone unprosecuted, but uncommented on altogether.

More importantly, and more imminently problematic, a potential armed response of the U.N. in response to an event that is ongoing can be quashed because permanent members disagree on whether or not an incident merits a response at all. For example, the Rwandan Genocide of 1994,[501] during which an estimated 500,000 - 650,000[502] ethnic Tutsi peoples were slaughtered by Hutu extremist militias in the aftermath of the assassination of the dictatorial President of Rwanda, Juvénal Habyarimana,[503] an event which took place in the context of a brutal civil war between the Rwandan

---

[501] U.N.S.C.. Res. 955, U.N. SCOR, 49th Sess, U.N.Doc. S/955, (Nov. 8th, 1994)

[502] André Guichaoua, *Counting the Rwandan Victims of War and Genocide: Concluding Reflections*, 22 Journal of Genocide Research 125–141 (2019).

[503] The Editors of Encyclopedia Britannica, Juvénal Habyarimana Encyclopedia Britannica (2022), https://www.britannica.com/biography/Juvenal-Habyarimana (last visited Apr 28, 2022).

Patriotic Front,[504] a Tutsi group, and the majority-Hutu government of Rwanda. Immediately in the aftermath of the assassination, Théoneste Bagosora, a colonel in the Rwandan Armed Forces, established a "crisis committee," which, paranoid of the supposed infiltration of the Tutsi into Rwandan society, and espousing the enthosupremicist ideology of "Hutu Power," massacred hundreds of thousands. The United Nations became aware of the genocide while it was in progress, as the U.N. Assistance Mission for Rwanda (UNAMIR),[505] a U.N. peacekeeping force, had been present in-country since 1993, but the Department of Peacekeeping Operations and the Security Council heavily restricted any armed response, as the mandate of UNAMIR was originally an observatory in nature. In fact, in a move widely seen as counterproductive, and directly enabling of the genocide, the Security Council voted in April of 1994[506] to immediately reduce the troop deployment level of UNAMIR to 250 soldiers and support personnel, a paltry number, even with the force multiplier produced by the advanced weaponry they possessed. Additionally, these troops were explicitly prohibited from intervening militarily, meaning even when the commander of the mission, Major General Roméo Antonius Dallaire,[507]

---

[504] Human Rights Watch, THE RWANDAN PATRIOTIC FRONT The Rwandan Patriotic Front (2022),
https://www.hrw.org/reports/1999/rwanda/Geno15-8-03.htm#:~:text=
The%20Rwandan%20Patriotic%20Front%20ended%20the%201994
%20genocide,began%20in%20early%20April%20and%20ended%20
in%20July.?msclkid=674f3196c70f11ec978dddf1e510d27a (last visited Apr 28, 2022).
[505] U.N.S.C.. Res. 872, U.N. SCOR, 49th Sess, U.N.Doc. S/872, (Oct. 5th, 1993)
[506] U.N.S.C.. Res. 912, U.N. SCOR, 49th Sess, U.N.Doc. S/912, (Apr. 21st, 1994)
[507] Peter Saracino, Roméo Dallaire

attempted to request permission to intervene, he was denied. Ostensibly, the Security Council took this position in an ill-guided attempt to reduce tensions, but it failed miserably, and the genocide occured in all of its depreved totality. British newspaper *The Guardian*, which had been covering the unfolding crisis, observed U.N. troops idly watching the genocide unfold, writing -

> A few yards from the French troops, a Rwandan woman was being hauled along the road by a young man with a machete. He pulled at her clothes as she looked at the foreign soldiers in the desperate, terrified hope that they could save her from her death. But none of the troops moved. 'It's not our mandate, 'said one, leaning against his jeep as he watched the condemned woman, the driving rain splashing at his blue United Nations badge.

The Security Council effectively dithered, debating back and forth the merits of involving the U.N., and in the end, of the members of the Council, only New Zealand supported more active engagement. Most other nations, especially the United States, took the position that this was a matter that was not of concern to them, and did not want to waste material or lives getting involved. This was due to political factors, and was a calculus that relied not on any measure of justice, or saving lives, but rather on expanding even a shadow of effort, which could have saved hundreds of thousands of lives. To this day, the Rwandan Genocide is recognized as perhaps the U.N.'s greatest failure, and illustrates the issue with possessing a top-down political system for justice and

---

Encyclopedia Britannica (2021), https://www.britannica.com/biography/Romeo-Dallaire (last visited Apr 28, 2022).

harm prevention. Subjectivity can be positive, but when objectivity is hobbled by selfish political concerns, the consequences prove fatal and traumatic, in this case for half a million Rwandans, and elsewhere for millions of other victims of international crimes.

THE END OF THE BEGINNING FOR *CASUS BELLI*

Casus belli, has, and always will be, an incredibly chimerical and fluid concept. The only thing that can be somewhat agreed upon is that casus foederis is more evidently sound, due to the nature of the act of joining a conflict as "performance" of a contract. However, whether or not a mutual defense treaty is sound at all times is debatable, and the legality of the original nation's response to an alleged event, which may itself call into question the legitimacy of invoking the pact, in turn calls into question the invocation of that defense compact. The issue in resolving the subjective nature of casus belli lies not in defining the concept, or even in getting nations to agree on that concept, but rather in the selective enforcement of any response when the legitimacy of a claim is called into question. For millennia, philosophers ranging from Aristotle to Aquinas have laid out their evolving views on what does and does not constitute a just war, and have attempted to present those views to scholars, the public, and the rulers of nations alike in an effort to shape not just national policy, but the international order. These concepts have evolved over time from merely a recognition and distinction of states as legally separate entities into the burgeoning and increasingly interconnected global community we live in today. Our development of international law as a codified body has continued on an exponentially swift scale over the past century, and yet, our enforcement of key laws designed to prevent acts of aggression, genocide, and war crimes is sorely lacking. It is lacking, not due to a lack of a legally enabled response, but rather because of selective enforcement by world powers that possess and wield a comparatively outsized amount of that power within the structure of institutions such as the United Nations and the International Criminal Court.

Noam Chomsky once said, "For the powerful, crimes are those that others commit."[508] These nations often reserve the right to ignore or disproportionately enforce international law, reflecting the principle of victor's justice; that powerful nations exert their brand of "justice" upon weaker states, simply by virtue of the fact that they are powerful. It is a gross miscarraige of justice and a blatant violation of the principle of due process that these nations are entitled to place their finger firmly upon the scales, and tip them to fit their geopolitical advantage. Primarily, this is enabled by the fact that the five great powers, having founded the United Nations, were granted the privilege to wield an outsized amount of influence within the U.N., in perpetuity, for as long as the United Nations is in existence. This has created a

---

[508] Noam Chomsky, *Wars of Aggression*, *in* Imperial Ambitions: Conversations with Noam Chomsky on the Post-9/11 World 73 (2006),
https://www.bing.com/ck/a?!&&p=94d148b930f92ca2186f675f8244
3e899fec53335aedf7e828290ce7285d084dJmltdHM9MTY1MTE4M
TMxMyMyZpZ3VpZD01M2Q4MjQ0Yy0yYzBjLTRlMDAtYTA2NS1
mMzM1Y2E0ZjI5NDEmaW5zaWQ9NTE2MA&ptn=3&fclid=27cfe
1b9-c73a-11ec-8cc0-5b51169d9252&u=a1aHR0cHM6Ly9saWJyYX
J5LnVuaXRlZGRpdmVyc2l0eS5jb29wL01vcmVmQm9va3NfYW5k
X1JlcG9ydHMvTm9hbV9DaG9tc2t5LUlttcGVyaWFsX0FtYml0aW9
ucy5wZGY_bXNjbGtpZD0yN2NmZTFiOWM3M2ExMWVjOGNj
MDViNTExNjlkOTI1Mg&ntb=1 (last visited Apr 28, 2022).

---

two-tiered class system, with the five nations above the rest. However, from an equitable, moral, and legal standpoint, there is no reason that any of these nations should be considered to be legally distinct from the other one-hundred-ninety on the planet. In fact, if the argument for this two-tiered system is one of power, and not of historical sentiment, then it is fallacious, as power structures frequently shift drastically, even over a short period of time. The U.N. is likely to exist for hundreds of years, if not millennia into the future, and assuming that the nations that are not currently members of the "permanent five" will never reach their geopolitical influence sometime in the future is a flawed assumption. As the United States, the world's policeman, only acquired that status over the course of the past century, it is reasonable to assume that it is plausible that other nations will eventually surpass it over the course of the U.N. 's lifetime. However, if the argument is not one of power, but one of historical sentiment, then that alone cannot be a justifiable reason for disenfranchising millions of people around the world insofar as equal justice is concerned. If equal justice, particularly in determining the laws and the cause of war, is to be applied, then it is essential that the nations of the world are treated as equal entities, both in terms of the level of scrutiny they receive and the power they possess to deflect that scrutiny. By amending the structure of the international governing bodies to reflect this, only then can we ensure that acts of aggression are halted, genocide is stopped in its tracks, and combatants and non-combatants alike are treated equitably, no matter the flag they fight for.

Casus belli is, and always has been the just cause of war, and though that definition may have changed over the past five thousand years of human history, we now as a species have identified what that term generally means. It is now on us to ensure that the teachings of scholars like Cicero, Grotius, Vitoria, and a myriad of others do not go wasted, that our ideals, however they are debated, are enforced consistently, and that we are ever evolving, toward equal justice for all. It is said that all wars are crimes, but certainly some are more criminal than others, and it is the duty of those international organizations that we have empowered with the means to ascertain that distinction, to do so, and in doing so, create not merely a better and more fair tomorrow, but thousands of better, fairer tomorrows, for the voiceless and the downtrodden, as well as for the powerful and the fortunate, rendering the dreams of equality of billions unto reality. Collectively, humanity, possessed of the means to rise to the occasion, must do this, not out of avarice or a desire to advance one's own interests, but as a declaration of the right for all humans to, in many cases, be treated as human at all. When the stakes can quite literally get no higher, we have the greatest responsibility to ensure that equal treatment before the law is the only product of our oversight. It may well be that all wars are crimes, but that does not mean that humanity's response must be criminal as well.

A HUMAN RIGHTS PERSPECTIVE ON THE ADVERSE IMPACT OF SANCTIONS: THE COVID-19 EPIDEMIC IN IRAN

BY ROZHINA AMINI

INTRODUCTION

At the 76th session of the United Nations General Assembly, Iranian president Ayatollah Seyyed Ebrahim Raisi, stated that sanctions are a modern form of warfare for the United States. President Raisi emphasized that sanctions, especially sanctions affecting public access to medicine at the time of the COVID-19 pandemic, are crimes against humanity.[509] Modern wars that feature sanctions and embargoes have been found to increasingly affect civilians, since they are not provided the typical war-related protections of typical violent

---

[509] President Ebrahim Raisi. UN General Assembly. (2022)

warfare.[510] Since the Islamic Revolution of 1979, U.S. imposed sanctions have had various effects on business, investment, trade, and public health in the country. Although humanitarian goods are specially exempted from sanctions, the provisions in place impact the availability of basic medications and production of supplies.[511] Martin Griffiths, Under-Secretary General for Humanitarian Affairs and Emergency Relief Coordinator, said urging the Council and Member States that "In all contexts, they should ensure that sanctions do not restrict the enjoyment of economic, social, and cultural rights including the right to food, water, shelter, and health".[512] Mitigating the humanitarian impact of sanctions in light of the COVID- 19 pandemic requires the international community to continue to review how sanctions are designed and implemented.

BACKGROUND ON THE IRANIAN ECONOMIC SANCTIONS REGIME

As an alternative to military action, sanctions have often been applied by nations and international organizations

---

[510] Garfield, R., Devin, J., & Fausey, J. (1995). The health impact of economic sanctions. *Bulletin of the New York Academy of Medicine*, *72*(2), 454–469.

[511] Butler, Declan. "Iran Hit by Drug Shortage: Sanctions Cause Increasing Shortfall in Medicines and Vaccines."Nature (London) 504, no. 7478 (2013): 15.

[512] UNSC. "Concerned by Unintended Negative Negative Impact of Sanctions, Speakers in Security Council Urge Action to Better Protect Civilians, Ensure Humanitarian Needs are Met" *Meetings Coverage and Press Releases.* (February 7 2022) Accessed March 27, 2022. https://www.un.org/press/en/2022/sc14788.doc.htm

as a policy tool to react to conflict.[513] Western governments, especially the United States, have long used sanctions and economic embargoes as a means of limiting development and trade to pressure the country into policy change. In regards to the Islamic Republic of Iran, decades-long comprehensive unilateral and multilateral economic sanctions have been in place by the United States and other bodies to oversee the actions of the regime. Sanctions have been a significant characteristic of U.S-Iran policy since the 1979 Islamic Revolution which ousted the monarch Mohammad Reza Shah, a prominent U.S ally.[514] Under the provisions of the 1977 International Emergency Economic Powers Act (IEEPA), President Carter enacted Executive Order 12170; freezing Iranian government assets in the United States in response to the U.S. Iran hostage crisis of 1979-1981.[515] Though President Carter was the first to enact an executive order under IEEPA he was not the last, as sanctions persisted with multiple objectives in order to address perceived threats from Iran. In the 1980s and 1990s, sanctions were intended to try to compel Iranian government officials to cease supporting acts of terrorism and to limit Iran's strategic power aspirations in the region; after the mid-2000s U.S and international sanctions have focused on limiting the actions of the Iranian nuclear program.[516]

Sanctions have only been intensified in the last decade because of the international community's uncertainty

---

[513] Davis L, Engerman S. History lessons: sanctions-neither war nor peace. *J Econ Perspect.* 2003;17(2):187–197.
[514] "Iran Sanctions" *Congressional Research Service,* (2022), 1-92.
[515] id.
[516] id.

about the proposed peaceful purpose of Iran's nuclear program and the inadequacy of trust-building actions of this country.[517] Since 2009 the Supreme Leader, Ayatollah Ali Khamenei, has maintained that "We fundamentally reject nuclear weapons, and prohibit the use and production of nuclear weapons" while also maintaining a rhetoric of enmity such as claiming that "With what tyranny the enemy camp is emphasizing our nuclear energy. They themselves know that we are not pursuing nuclear weapons and that we are only trying to benefit from peaceful nuclear energy".[518] Multilateral sanctions applied at the end of 2011 and strengthened between 2012 and 2015 brought immense pressure on the country, resulting in an all time low in the value of Iranian currency.[519] In 2015 the Joint Comprehensive Plan (JCPOA) was drafted as an international agreement with Iran and the P5 + 1 states of the United Nations Security Council (UNSC) in which sanctions were temporarily lifted. However, in 2018 the US pulled out of the JCPOA and sanctions were re-imposed. [520]

---

[517] Kokabisaghi F. Assessment of the Effects of Economic Sanctions on Iranians' Right to Health by Using Human Rights Impact Assessment Tool: A Systematic Review. Int J Health Policy Manag. (2018):374-393.

[518] Khamenei, Ali. "If we retreat from peaceful nuclear energy, country's development will be impeded" *Khamenei. IR.* Accessed February 22, 2022.
https://english.khamenei.ir/news/8865/If-we-retreat-from-peaceful-nuclear-energy-country-s-development

[519] Cordesman, A. H., B. Gold, S. Khazai, and B. Bosserman. "Sanctions, Energy, Arms Control, and Regime Change." *Center for Strategic & International Studies,* 2012.

[520] OFAC. "May 2018 Guidance on Reimposing Certain Sanctions in Respect to Iran." *U.S Department of The Treasury.* Accessed April 6, 2022.
https://home.treasury.gov/policy-issues/financial-sanctions/san

American scholar William Beeman has argued that the Iranians have, since before the revolution, been engaged in a symbolic discourse which emphasizes resistance as a means of establishing and maintaining revolutionary credentials of anti-imperialism and a correct moral posture on the international scene.[521] Iran's perception of the United States in particular as the enemy is greatly shaped by its self-image as a subjugated great power, officials often cite the country's historical relationship particularly the 1953 Iranian coup d'état (as referred to as the 28 Mordad coup d'état) overthrowing the democratically elected Prime minister Mohammad Mosaddegh in favor for the monarchical rule of Mohammad Reza Pahlavi as reasoning for its position as a state enemy.[522] Despite factional disputes, the Iranian government across multiple presidential administrations has shown resilience in the face of international pressure to halt their pursuit of nuclear research maintaining the position that it is their right as a sovereign nation.[523] The motivations of the Islamic Republic to enrich uranium is ideological contested across the international community for decades and in that time, it was estimated that Iran

---

ctions-programs-and-country-information/iran-sanctions/re-im position-of-the-sanctions-on-iran-that-had-been-lifted-or-waiv ed-under-the-jcpoa

[521] Beeman, William. "Images of the Great Satan: „ Representations of the United States in the Iranian Revolution, in *Religion and Politics in Iran: Shi'ism from Quietism to Revolution*, ed.

[522] Dobbins, James. Alireza Nader, Dalia Dassa Kaye, and Frederic Wehrey. "Iran's Interests, Objectives, and Strategies." In *Coping with a Nuclearizing Iran*, 2011. 10-11.

[523] Siavoshi, Sussan. "Factionalism and Iranian Politics: The Post-Khomeini Experience." Iranian studies 25, no. 3-4 (1992): 27–49.

has lost over 1 trillion dollars due to economic damage caused from unilateral sanctions imposed by the United States, this economic stress is felt by the Iranian public since inflation is crippling their economy.[524]

HEALTH CRISIS IN LIGHT OF COVID-19

On February 19, 2020, the Iran Ministry of Health announced its first confirmed cases of infection in the central province of Qom.[525] By March 12, 2020, the World Health Organization (WHO) had announced the COVID-19 pandemic, its rapid outbreak and level of transmission proved a public health emergency of international concern.[526] According to Iran's Ministry of Health and the WHO, as of February 25, 2022 there has been at least 7,011,932 confirmed cases of COVID-19 with 135,952 deaths; as of February 27, 2022 a total of 140,619,255 vaccine doses have been administered.[527] It must be stressed that the real numbers of COVID-19 infections and related deaths are far higher than official reporting due to the ministry's adherence to WHO protocols that require a positive PCR test result for

---

[524] Maziar Motamedi. "US Sanctions Inflicted $1 Trillion Damage on Iran's Economy: FM." Nuclear Energy News. Al Jazeera. February 21, 2021.

[525] "Iran Reports Its First 2 Cases of the New Coronavirus". *New York Times*. Accessed February 26, 2022. https://archive.ph/CuAQZ

[526] Timeline of WHO's response to COVID-19. Accessed February 26, 2022. https://www.who. int/news-room/detail/29-06-2020-covidtimeline.

[527] "Iran (Islamic Republic of): WHO Coronavirus Disease (Covid-19) Dashboard with Vaccination Data." World Health Organization. World Health Organization. Accessed February 26, 2022. https://covid19.who.int/region/emro/country/ir.

reporting.[528] Iran's repressive leadership has also been criticized for their reporting and mismanagement of data regarding the extent of the virus's spread and the death toll within the first year of the pandemic. Of the fifthteen countries with the highest number of recorded cases to date, Iran is the poorest alongside Vietnam, impeding their ability to respond to the pandemic.[529]

The sanctions on Iran have caused a fall in the country's revenues, devaluation of national currency, and increase of inflation and unemployment, yet the impact of sanctions against the banking and financial sector is of utmost importance here. Blocking of Iran's main banking infrastructure and cutting the country off from the Worldwide Interbank Financial Telecommunication (SWIFT) has created innumerable obstacles for international trade of which humanitarian goods, such as medicine, is no exception.[530] In December 2020 Iranian Foreign Minister Mohammad Javad Zarud claimed that U.S. financial sanctions were preventing Iran from making an initial advance payment to the COVID-19 Vaccines Global Access Facility or Covax, which the WHO designed to ensure a more equitable distribution of coronavirus vaccines.[531] Once talks to revive the

[528] Mehr News Agency. "Real numbers of deaths are two times higher than the official reports." Accessed February 26, 2022. http://mehrnews.com/xSVqp.
[529] id.
[530] Namazi, Siamak. "Sanctions and Medical Supply Shortages in Iran" *Wilson Center Viewpoints* No.20, (February 2013).
[531] Berger, Miriam. "US Sanctions could impede Iran's access to coronavirus vaccines, experts say." *The Washington Post,* (December 7, 2020) Accessed February 26, 2022 https://www.washingtonpost.com/world/middle_east/iran-covax-coronavirus-vaccine-sanctions/2020/12/07/61a721f8-3632-11eb-9699-00d311f13d2d_story.html

nuclear deal faltered, mistrust against the West intensified, pushing the Conservative faction to intensify anti-Western rhetoric. In January of 2021, Ayatollah Ali Khamenei forbade the import of Western shots, going against the efforts of Iranian health and banking officials to ensure Iran's access to global coronavirus treatments.[532] Iran has primarily relied on Sinopharm, the state-backed Chinese vaccine and its own COVIran Barekat, but has opened up access to AstraZeneca (British-Swedish), Sputnik V (Russian), Covaxin (Indian), but experienced this access nearly a year after many other states.[533]

The COVID-19 pandemic has occurred at a time of unprecedented economic crisis in Iran, in which shortages and high prices of life saving medical supplies.[534] Although essential medicines and medical equipment are technically exempt from sanctions, studies show that their availability is restricted by the effect of sanctions on manufacturing and trade capacity impacting the entire commercial sector. Kheirandish et al. conducted a time series study assessing the effect of sanctions on drugs for noncommunicable diseases (NCDs) such as diabetes, asthma, cancer, and multiple sclerosis; finding that market availability of 13 of 26 drugs were significantly

---

[532] Cunningham, Erin. "Iran's Khamenei bans the import of U.S. and U.K. coronavirus vaccines." *The Washington Post,* (December 7, 2020) Accessed February 26, 2022 https://www.washingtonpost.com/world/2021/01/08/iran-khamenei-bans-us-uk-coronavirus-vaccines/
[533] NPR. "Iran is undergoing a mass vaccination campaign as omicron loom
[534] Gorji, A. "Medical supplies in Iran hit by sanctions." *Nature* 495, (2013).

reduced.[535] Their findings are supported by multiple studies that find that the claim that sanctions only target political aspects does not acknowledge the hardship experienced by civilians.[536] It is estimated that the probability of novel disease outbreaks like COVID-19 will likely grow three times in the next three decades, making it essential that action be taken to solve vaccine inequality in the world. [537]

HUMAN RIGHTS DIMENSION

Humanitarian goods and necessities such as medicine are technically exempted from sanctions imposed by the United Nations, the United States, and the European Union following the standards defined by internationally recognized human rights documents.[538] The Universal Declaration of Human Rights of 1948 (UDHR), the International Covenant on Economic, Social, and

---

[535] Kheirandish, Mehrnaz, Vida Varahrami, Abbas Kebriaeezade, and Abdol Majid Cheraghali. "Impact of Economic Sanctions on Access to Noncommunicable Diseases Medicines in the Islamic Republic of Iran." *Eastern Mediterranean Health Journal* 24, no. 1 (2018): 42–51.
[536] Garfield R. The impact of economic sanctions on health and well-being. Overseas Development Institute; (1999).
Ioana M. Petrescu, *The Humanitarian Impact of Economic Sanctions*, 10 EUROPOLITY: CONTINUITY & CHANGE EUR. GOVERNANCE 205 (2016).
[537] Penn, Micheal. "Statistics Say Large Pandemics are More Likely than We Thought" *Duke: Global Health Institute* (August 23, 2021) Accessed March 27, 2022. https://globalhealth.duke.edu/news/statistics-say-large-pandemics-are-more-likely-we-thought
[538] Butler, Declan. "Iran Hit by Drug Shortage: Sanctions Cause Increasing Shortfall in Medicines and Vaccines." *Nature* 504, no. 7478 (2013): 15.

Cultural Rights of 1966 (ICESCR), and the International
Covenant on Political and Civil Rights of 1966 (ICPCR),
all recognize the right to adequate health and medicine.
Article 25 of the UDHR refers to a person's right to a
standard of living adequate for the health and well-being
of them and their family, this includes the right to
medicine.[539] Article 12 of the ICESCR in turn refers to
the right to the highest attainable standard of physical
and mental health .[540] The UN's Committee of
Economic, Social, and Cultural Rights have expressed
concerns regarding sanctions as early as 1997, adopting
a general comment that sanctions almost always have a
dramatic impact on the rights recognized by the
ICESCR, frequently causing significant disruption in the
distribution of humanitarian goods such as
pharmaceuticals.[541] The UN Human Rights Council in
2013 declared that there is reliable evidence about
serious consequences of sanctions on the rights of
people, particularly vulnerable groups such as women,
children, the elderly, the poor, minorities, indigenous
people and persons living with disabilities.[542] Even
though the provisions of the Declaration are widely
regarded as the ideals of human rights law, a glaring
issue proves itself in implementation. The UDHR, in
itself, is not binding on member states. President Jimmy
Carter signed the ICESCR in 1977 yet the United States

---

[539] UN General Assembly. Universal Declaration of Human
Rights; 1948
[540] UN General Assembly. International Covenant on
Economic, Social and Cultural Rights. United Nations; 1966.
[541] UN General Assembly. International Covenant on
Economic, Social and Cultural Rights. United Nations; 1997.
[542] UN Human Rights Council. Human rights and unilateral
coercive measures (24/14). New York: UN General Assembly;
2013.

has yet to ratify it.[543] However, due to such widespread ratification across 171 states, the ICESCR is considered customary international law and can legally bind states regardless of ratification. [544] The United States is therefore required to commit to the protection of the right to health established by the ICESCR.

The constitution of the World Health Organization (WHO), states a right to the highest attainable standard of health - The health of all human beings is defined by them as a necessary condition to the attainment of universal peace.[545] In 2005 the WHO rewrote its International Health Regulations, in order to implement rules and regulations on all member states to build a collective defense against global health challenges, and improve pandemic preparedness and response.[546] In November of 2021 Tedros Adhanom Ghebreyesus, WHO Director General, emphasized that its Constitution to which binds its members affirms "that the health of all peoples is fundamental to the attainment of peace and security, and is dependent upon the fullest cooperation of individuals and States".[547]

---

[543] Kinney, Eleanor D."The International Human Right to Health: What Does this Mean for Our Nation and World," Indiana Law Review 34, no. 4 (2001): 1457-1476
[544] id.
[545] World Health Organization. Constitution of the World Health Organization. World Health Organization; 1960.
[546] Council on Foreign Relations. "Major Epidemics of the Modern Era" Accessed March 27, 2022. https://www.cfr.org/timeline/major-epidemics-modern-era
[547] World Health Organization. "WHO Director- General's opening remarks at the Special Session of the World Health Assembly" (November 29, 2021) Accessed March 27, 2022. https://www.who.int/director-general/speeches/detail/who-dire

CONCLUSION

As aforementioned, more novel disease outbreaks like COVID-19 are expected within the next 50 years making it imperative for the international community to review how sanctions are designed and implemented. Although legal and deemed necessary to respond to actions of the Islamic Republic of Iran, the decades-long economic sanctions regime led by the United States has had a severe public health impact, leading to poor health outcomes among Iranian civilians. There is no doubt that this crisis is exacerbated by the shortcomings of the Iranian government and their anatognizism towards the West. Yet low income countries are disproportionately affected by infectious disease spillover events, leaving them at the front lines of pandemic threats.[548] This pandemic has hit the world in an unprecedented way proving that the international community must move to end vaccination inequality despite geopolitical concerns.

---

ctor-general-s-opening-remarks-at-the-special-session-of-the-world-health-assembly---29-november-2021
[548] Smitham, Eleni. Glassman, Amanda. "The Next Pandemic Could Come Soon and Be Deadlier" *Center for Global Development.* (August 25, 2021) Accessed March 27, 2022. https://www.cgdev.org/blog/the-next-pandemic-could-come-soon-and-be-deadlier

THE AMERICAN UNIVERSITY
UNDERGRADUATE LAW JOURNAL

AU UNDERGRAD
LAW JOURNAL

LEGAL THEORY

COLUMN

LEGAL INTERPRETATIONS: COMMON LAW AND THE CONSTITUTION

BY SEBASTIAN MAHAL

INTRODUCTION

Do we, in America, wish to have a "living Constitution"? This question has been at the forefront of legal theory since the coinage of the term but has yet to be resolved. A living constitution, according to David A. Strauss of The University of Chicago Law School, is "one that evolves, changes over time, and adapts to new circumstances, without being formally amended."[549] Upon reading the definition, one must believe that yes—the U.S. Constitution must be a living document. The Bill of Rights was ratified over 230 years ago. In that time, our country has undergone innumerable changes. Notably, its population has multiplied a hundred times over, not to mention the drastic cultural,

---

[549] Strauss, David A. "The University of Chicago Law School." The Living Constitution | University of Chicago Law School, September 17, 2010. https://www.law.uchicago.edu/news/living-constitution.

economic, and technological changes across the United
States.

So an ever-changing interpretation of the Constitution
that fits the times is a necessary and popular approach,
right? Well, it may come as a surprise to hear that some
of the most famous Supreme Court justices, including
Justices Antonin Scalia[550] and Clarence Thomas[551], were
vehemently opposed to this methodology. "Originalism"
or "original meaning," defined by the Congressional
Research Services' *Modes of Constitutional
Interpretation*, is considering "the meaning of the
Constitution as understood by at least some segment of
the populace at the time of the Founding."[552] The first
appearance of the expression can be found in an article
by legal scholar Paul Brest in 1981[553] and has been
pivotal in framing the discussion of how the Constitution
is read and understood.

---

[550] Patel, Ushma. "Scalia Favors 'Enduring,' Not Living,
Constitution." Princeton University. The Trustees of Princeton
University, December 11, 2012.
https://www.princeton.edu/news/2012/12/11/scalia-favors-end
uring-not-living-constitution.
[551] Magnet, Myron. "Clarence Thomas and the Lost
Constitution." Manhattan Institute, September 30, 2019.
https://www.manhattan-institute.org/speech-clarence-thomas-l
ost-constitution.
[552] Murrill, Brandon J. "Modes of Constitutional
Interpretation." Congressional Research Service, March 15,
2018. https://sgp.fas.org/crs/misc/R45129.pdf.
[553] Solum, Lawrence B. "What Is Originalism? The Evolution
of Contemporary Originalist Theory - Georgetown Law."
Georgetown University Law Center, 2011.
https://scholarship.law.georgetown.edu/cgi/viewcontent.cgi?ar
ticle=2362&context=facpub.

Brest, a former dean and professor at The Stanford Law School, posted an article on the subject of originalism in the Westlaw legal database in 1981. In this document, he makes a handful of arguments as to why an originalist approach is not just the better but the *only* valid viewpoint for Constitutional interpretation. Brest argues that our Constitution is designed to be the unfaltering foundation of our democracy, informing the courts as well as the citizens of their rights and responsibilities. If judges were capable of deciding on a whim whether to consider the document or ignore it, the Constitution would be entirely undermined.[554] Since then, Brest and other critics of the living Constitution have done an impressive job stigmatizing the term, leading to the oversight of the methodology in scholarly journals and legal proceedings.

So, how does one battle the contradicting sentiments: wanting a fluid, adaptable Constitution that is able to change when society deems necessary, while also wanting to maintain the document's power and strength? Strauss, cited earlier, argues for another practice in this discussion: common law.

WHAT IS COMMON LAW

Common law, defined by The Cornell Law School, is "law that is derived from judicial decisions instead of

---

[554] Barnett, Randy. "Opinion | Presenting a 'Unified' Theory of Originalism." *The Washington Post*, WP Company, 23 Oct. 2021, https://www.washingtonpost.com/news/volokh-conspiracy/wp/2017/10/08/presenting-a-unified-theory-of-originalism/.

from statutes."[555] Instead of being built upon "authoritative, foundational, quasi-sacred"[556] texts like the U.S. Constitution, the common law can be developed through legal precedents or by analogy to corresponding areas of law. This principle provides a society with the advantages of living constitutionalism—through leaving room for change and adjustment—as well as originalism—through placing restrictions in the form of historical precedent. The United States may not have been able to rely on a common law approach to justice during its inception, but after nearly 250 years of legal suits, it is decidedly mature enough today to respect the basis of other legal cases and to inform the future ones.

One of the strongest arguments for common law is how it develops evolutionarily, in the same way a society does. The Constitution, at the time it was written, was not very democratic. Only white males were permitted to vote and enslavement was tolerated. Also, state representatives voted to ratify the document, not the citizens of the respective states. If we read the Constitution in the exact way it was ratified, we would still be living according to the rules and norms of the 1780s and necessary progress would be halted. Instead, under a common law system, one cannot ascertain the content of the law by one single document. Common law allows for the law of today to be informed by the law of past precedential decisions, better grasping the

---

[555] Wex Definitions Team. "Common Law." Legal Information Institute. Cornell Law School, May 2020.
https://www.law.cornell.edu/wex/common_law.
[556] Strauss, David A. "The University of Chicago Law School." The Living Constitution | University of Chicago Law School, September 17, 2010.
https://www.law.uchicago.edu/news/living-constitution.

ever-changing conventions of a society. Modern interpreters and judges would promote this evolution simply by continuing it. This would lead to an evolving living practice that legal professionals could follow rather than one that imposes on our original legal documents.

Here is an example of how this evolution may play out. When a judge is met with a difficult legal decision, they will undoubtedly look at how earlier courts resolved similar disputes. After centuries of intermingling precedents in this country's history, it is very likely that the judge will be able to find an analogous case. But if they are unable to, or if earlier cases do not closely enough resemble the current dispute, common law grants that judge the power to insert their own judgment and set the precedent for future legal cases.[557] What must inform the judge's decisions are cultural and social sentiments of the time, so as to maintain the importance of the legal cases into the future.

One may argue that this is a possible overreach by lower courts in the U.S., as it is letting the perception of one judge empower legal decisions for decades to come. To this argument, one must remember that in any properly running system of law, the vast majority of potential cases should not even reach the courts to begin with.[558]

---

[557] "Common Law." Wikipedia. Wikimedia Foundation, March 2, 2022.
https://en.wikipedia.org/wiki/Common_law#Common_law_na
tional_legal_systems_today.
[558] Coan, Andrew. "Duke Law Journal." Living Constitutional Theory | Duke Law Journal, June 2017.
https://dlj.law.duke.edu/2017/06/living-constitutional-theory/#
BTL_ftn50.

This safety net should be issued in part due to a strong intertwined collection of precedent. As Strauss writes, the law should be "so clear that people do not dispute it, and that is true of common law systems, too."[559] And regardless, even when the decision in a difficult legal case is unclear, those historical precedents "will limit the possible outcomes that a judge can reach."[560]

CONCLUSION

Living constitutionalism is oftentimes written off as too ambiguous, "too manipulable"[561]—these critiques may very well be true. Originalism relies on the argument that there is no realistic opponent to the theory. Strauss claims that "originalism requires judges and lawyers to be historians."[562] Conversely, common law requires judges and lawyers to be just that: judges and lawyers. To reason from precedent and sparingly add one's own perception seems to be a much more dependable system than relying on a dated paper located deep in the National Archives.

Even a card-carrying originalist can concede that the collected wisdom of those that came before us is vital in having a complete understanding of our legal system. Those people were engrossed with solving the same problems that we are today. This attitude is exactly why a precedential legal methodology makes sense,

---

[559] Strauss, David A. "The University of Chicago Law School." The Living Constitution | University of Chicago Law School, September 17, 2010.
https://www.law.uchicago.edu/news/living-constitution.
[560] Ibid.
[561] Ibid.
[562] Ibid.

"especially if the precedents are clear and have been established for a long time."[563] There is a convincing argument for our legal decisions to be informed by the basis of cases months and years prior to us. There is not such a strong case for the decisions of those who lived in the 1700s.

---

[563] Ibid.

SOVEREIGNTY AND COLONIALISM: TREATIES BETWEEN INDIGENOUS TRIBES AND THE UNITED STATES GOVERNMENT

BY PHOEBE HOLMAN

INTRODUCTION

Law schools in the United States teach two main types of law: federal and state. The legislative, executive, and judicial branches, as well as the text of the United States Constitution, are some of the first things students learn during their education. But another type of law exists that governs over one million people living within drawn borders of the country. Tribal law, used by indigenous tribes in the United States, is completely separate from the U.S. Constitution and federal Indian law. The codes govern the interactions between tribes and the federal and state governments. Tribal law is complex and specific to each of the more than five hundred federally recognized tribes across the nation. The treaties that establish it are also complex, and the nature of their existence and legality is often completely ignored in the status quo for law education in the United States.

According to Assistant Professor at the Stanford Law School Elizabeth Reese, part of the Nambé Pueblo tribe and the school's first Native American faculty member, tribal law refers to the "kind of law that is passed by a tribal government and that applies on their land and to–in varying degrees–the persons on that land."[564] The indigenous population in the US is largely ignored by mainstream institutions as a way of silencing its people. Providing a well rounded education on tribal law will prepare students for working with Native American communities, and provide a nuanced and accurate understanding of the interactions between the United States government and the indigenous tribes whose land it occupies.

LEGAL FUNCTION

The way that indigenous tribes are represented in the Constitution has changed throughout the history of the United States. Prior to the Civil War, tribes were recognized as the western perception of sovereign nations, entirely separate from the States. The relationship between the two was governed by treaties, similar to agreements made between the United States and foreign nations. Often, these terms included ending wars, allocating territories, and settling other similar disputes. During the early founding of the federal

---

[564] Interview with Elizabeth A. Reese, Yunpoví, J.D. Assistant Prof. of Law, Stanford Law School. (Oct 7, 2021) (transcript available online, *High Country News*).

government and into American westward expansion, treaties were employed by the U.S. government to establish borders and territories with the indigenous tribes. Though they are often left to the side with legal education, these treaties are very much alive today and still govern the interactions between the United States and sovereign tribes today over their territories and rights.

Indigenous tribes are mentioned three times in the United States Constitution: Article I, Section 2, Clause 3, Article I, Section 8, and Section 2 of the Fourteenth Amendment. Section 2 of Article I stated that Native Americans would not be counted in the population of states when determining the apportionment of representatives in Congress. This was later appealed by the Fourteenth Amendment, meaning that, since its ratification in 1868, they are now counted when determining a state's allocated representatives (however, this does not mean that issues don't arise in properly representing the needs of tribes in Congress). Section 8 of Article I covers commerce, and gives Congress the power to regulate trade with tribes: "[The Congress shall have Power . . .] To regulate Commerce with foreign Nations, and among the several States, and with the Indian Tribes..."[565] These are the only places in the Constitution that directly mention the indigenous peoples.

Much can be told about the founders' views by the treaties that were employed by the colonizers after the formation of the government. An interesting example of this is the 1778 Treaty With the Delawares. This was the first official treaty recognized by the US. This treaty

---

[565] U.S. Const. art. I, § 8.

actually promised Congressional representation (among many other things, including that the land of the Delaware tribe would not be encroached upon by citizens of the United States). It also included a convenient statement at the end: "Provided, nothing contained in this article to be considered as conclusive until it meets with the approbation of Congress."[566] This treaty, as well as the rest, have been ignored many times by the government of the United States.

The encroachment of settlers on Indigenous land, as well as violent altercations involving colonizers attempting to expand and take protected resources, invalidated the terms of treaties many times. The 1782 attack on the Lenape tribe living under the Treaty of Fort Pitt[567], during which over ninety of those belonging to the Lenape tribe were killed, incorrectly accused of attacks on colonizers. After the massacre, white settlers continued to move on to lands allocated to the Lenape. Despite this, indigenous tribes continue to live under these Constitutional provisions and treaties today.

VALIDITY OF TREATIES

Many debate the validity of these treaties for a variety of reasons: constant, repeated violations of the terms on the part of the United States government, language barriers during the signing, the threat of force, and, of course, the fact that the settler colonialists setting up the treaties

---

[566] Treaty With the Delawares, Sept. 17, 1778, Senate Cmte. on Indian Affairs.
[567] Broken Treaties with Native American Tribes: Timeline History.com ,
https://www.history.com/news/native-american-broken-treaties (last visited Apr 6, 2022)

were already invading and annexing the territory that the tribes lived on before the treaties were signed. In the Supreme Court case Lone Wolf v. Hitchcock[568](1903), the Chief of the Kiowa tribe, sued the United States government for violations of the Medicine Lodge Treaty of 1867[569], which allocated land and resources, as well as providing guidelines for interactions between the U.S. and the Indigenous peoples. The Chief stated that the tribe had been defrauded when the United States altered the treaty when the US federal government seized two million acres of the reservation without the consent or consultation of the tribe). Lone Wolf appealed to the Supreme Court, which ruled that Congress' plenary power allowed them to violate treaties with indigenous tribes. This decision set a dangerous precedent that allowed the United States to continue to seize land and alter the terms of past treaties.

The validity of this SCOTUS decision is heavily debated: how can a treaty be considered a reasonable authority if they are continuously altered without the consent of or input from half of the involved parties? The concept of the plenary power, or absolute authority, of Congress to alter treaties like this, brings into question the justification of having a treaty in the first place. Absolute power over the control of the lands and resources of the Native American tribes inherently breaks all the treaties made with each of them, as well as depriving them of the things necessary for their survival. A treaty that is not enforced and constantly violated has no authority, and cannot be considered valid.

---

[568] Lone Wolf v. Hitchcock, 187 US 553 (Supreme Court of the U.S. 1903).
[569] Medicine Lodge Treaty, Oct. 21, 1867, Senate Cmte. on Indian Affairs.

FINAL THOUGHTS

Numerous harms of this deliberate gap in both historical and contemporary legal education can be observed in American society today. Dismissing an entire population's sovereignty and subsequently their legal system creates an inaccurate version of United States history and allows for indigenous peoples to be repeatedly underrepresented, oppressed, and forced off of their ancestral lands. Ignoring the teaching of the tribes' governments and sovereignty in legal education is a deliberate attempt to enforce the system of brutal oppression that exists within the United States government. It undermines the authority of what are essentially separate nations within the borders of the country, and creates the conditions for SCOTUS decisions like Lone Wolf v. Hitchcock. Establishing that Congress has the ability to violate these treaties whenever, without the consent of the tribes, renders them invalid, because they are not enforced at all.

THE LOSS OF THE ESTABLISHMENT CLAUSE AND ITS COMPREHENSIVE HISTORY

BY ABBIE KITARIEV

INTRODUCTION

When deciding Supreme Court cases there are a few different ways of looking at it; through an originalist lens which dictates that decisions should be made based on the original intention of the framers and living constitutionalism which extends the original meaning of the Constitution to be applicable to the current needs of the government and the people.

America itself was founded on religious liberty, it was a land of immigrants escaping religious persecution therefore in the bedrock of the Constitution is this intention to protect religion from government in the First Amendment. But the further into the future America goes the harder it has been to determine what is protecting religious liberty and what is the overtake of religion on the government. The Establishment Clause strictly states "Congress shall make no law respecting an establishment of religion, or prohibiting the free exercise thereof"[570] But what does that actually mean, and how does this clause not only protect religion but also protect the government from religion?

JEFFERSON AND THE CONSTITUTION

The Constitution is an astounding document; it has upheld America's democracy for hundreds of years yet as impressive as the document is, it has flaws. One of the fatal flaws of the Constitution was not restricting religious influence over the state enough. When the framers were first drafting the Constitution it was drafted as a godless document. Many pushed for a religious document citing that they did not want to run the government alongside pagans and Jews. But it has become apparent that the intention of the framers was to protect the religious liberty of all by writing the Establishment Clause because it allowed for religious freedom of every person and the Free Exercise Clause goes alongside that. If the budding nation allowed for one official established religion it would defeat the purpose of this free nation as it would allow for the persecution of those not practicing the official state-mandated religion. Another aspect of why the Constitution is so reserved in how much it talks about religion is that philosophers during that time which influenced the framers' writing of the Constitution viewed the church as a private matter and that any elected official should not vote or write bills because of their religious beliefs.[571] Jefferson even wrote about the

---

[570] U.S. Const.. amend. I
[571] L.S, Smith, *Religion, Politics, and the Establishment Clause: Does God Belong in American Public Life?*. 10 Chap.

separation of church and state in his letter to the
Danbury Baptist Church which has become famous for
its contents. He talks about the Establishment Clause and
the Free Exercise Clause in the First Amendment saying
that in his belief it will lead to the separation of church
and state and will "tend to restore to man all his natural
rights."[572] The framers never expected that religion could
overtake government which was visible in how Jefferson
and many other framers at the time often had prayer
sessions in the House of Representatives and many other
government buildings such as the Treasury
Department[573]. So when writing the establishment clause
and free exercise clause it was from the view of religious
rather than governmental protections.

EVERSON V. BOARD OF EDUCATION
OF THE TOWNSHIP OF EWING

However in the 20th century the position of religious
institutions began to change, taking on a more involved
approach to government starting in the 1940s with a
New Jersey Law authorizing the reimbursement by local
school boards for transportation costs to and from
schools. This reimbursement also covered private
schools 96% of which were parochial Catholic schools
that were receiving the benefits. A citizen by the name of

L. Rev. 299,
(2007),https://digitalcommons.chapman.edu/cgi/viewcontent.c
gi?article=1106&context=chapman-law-review
[572] Thomas Jefferson, *Jefferson's Letter to the Danbury
Baptists The Final Letter, as Sent*, (1802),
https://www.loc.gov/loc/lcib/9806/danpre.html
[573] Madison, P.A. *Misunderstanding Jefferson's 'Wall of
Separation' Metaphor,* (2010),
http://www.federalistblog.us/2010/11/_defending_jeffersons_
wall_of_separation_metaphor/.

Arch R. Everson sued New Jersey over the law as it was an indirect aid of religion coming out of his taxes. The case went up to the Supreme Court where it was decided that the law did not go against the Constitution as the money did not go directly to the parochial schools. This law was in fact enacted to support parents in sending their children to school[574]. The case itself was fairly simple but left the court divided and even though the court voted in favor of the reimbursement it set the first precedent of what the Establishment Clause defends.

Many argue that the decision Chief Justice Black wrote was a form of judicial activism as it reinterpreted Jefferson's letter to the Danbury Baptist Church and wrote a more elaborate Establishment Clause. Below is the decision that Chief Justice Black wrote:

> "Neither a state nor the Federal Government can set up a church. Neither can pass laws that aid one religion, aid all religions, or prefer one religion over another. Neither can force nor influence a person to go to or to remain away from church against his will or force him to profess a belief or disbelief in any religion. No person can be punished for entertaining or professing religious beliefs or disbeliefs, for church attendance, or non-attendance. No tax in any amount, large or small, can be levied to support any religious activities or institutions, whatever they may be called, or whatever form they may adopt to teach or practice religion. Neither a state nor the Federal Government can, openly or secretly, participate in the affairs of any religious organizations or groups and vice versa. In the words of Jefferson, the clause against establishment of religion by law was intended

---

[574] *Everson v. Board of Education of the Township of Ewing*, Oyez, https://www.oyez.org/cases/1940-1955/330us1 (last visited Apr 4, 2022).

to erect "a wall of separation between church and state.[575]"

This case continued to set a strong precedent for thirty years as to what the Establishment Clause was truly saying but it was a short-lived victory as in the next forty years the Establishment Clause began to slowly revert back to its original language.

For some time it seemed as though the separation of church and state would continue to be strong as the Everson case upheld the precedent for thirty years. Once Lemon v. Kurtzman came into the Supreme Court, the justices laid out a whole rulebook as to what constituted a violation of the Establishment Clause, it mandated that

"(1) a statute have a secular purpose,

(2) there be no evidence that the statute's principal effect is to advance or to inhibit religion, and

(3) the statute does not foster excessive entanglement between government and religion."[576]

This Lemon Test held strong at first but in ten years the court began to selectively apply the Lemon Test. In Lynch v. Donnely Justice O'Connor suggested that the Lemon test be modified as an endorsement test and that same modification was used in McCreary County v. American Civil Liberties Union of Ky. The endorsement test was not much different but allowed for a little

---

[575] L.S, Smith. *"Religion, Politics, and the Establishment Clause: Does God Belong in American Public Life?"*. 10 Chap. L. Rev. 299, (2007).
[576] L.S, Smith. *"Religion, Politics, and the Establishment Clause: Does God Belong in American Public Life?"*. 10 Chap. L. Rev. 299, (2007).

contribution to religion as long as the state did not objectively endorse it.

The decisions began to weaken even more after that until Lee *v.* Weisman supplied a coercion test which essentially stated that schools could not hire religious figures to speak because it coerced people into participating since anything that isn't actively speaking out against the religious speech was complacency in the act of listening.

The problem with all this isn't the new tests that were made, but with their selective approach to using the tests. It is strange to see how in Lee *v.* Weisman the court ruled that having religious speech in a school was unconstitutional but in a similar case such as Marsh *v.* Chambers ruled that a Chaplin could be hired using public funds to speak before legislative sessions. This selective approach has only become more frequent in recent years and is likely to continue to become even more frequent as the precedent begins to weaken towards the original words of the Constitution being simply that Congress can not establish a religion.[577]

POSSIBLE RESOLUTION

Unfortunately as this paper has shown the Establishment Clause has not been in decay; the fact of the matter is that in the Everson case Chief Justice Black set a precedent for the interpretation of the Constitution and twisted Jefferson's words to prevent the overtake of religion. Though the intention was good and necessary, it was a temporary fix to a long term problem that has been on the rise in American politics. Jefferson's own

---

[577] *Ibid.*, 333-335

intention of the Establishment Clause was not so much to prevent the government from being overtaken by religion as it was to prevent the overtake of religion by the government. Though the government can not allow for an official religion nothing is stopping any government official from voting, writing bills, and pursuing an agenda based on his religious beliefs and that includes justices whose most important precedent is set by the Constitution which only says no official establishment of religion. The establishment clause in the American Constitution has therefore not been in decay; the only thing that has been decaying is Chief Justices Black's interpretation of it and religious people's own belief in separating themselves from politics. The Republican Party becoming the party of the Moral Majority is a big issue for the American people's liberties in general as it applies to LGBT rights, women's rights, and minority religions rights but it is by no means behaving unlawfully as their goal is not an official establishment of a religion but a ruling through religious morality.

One of the ways to fix the issue of the Constitution being too vague and the precedent weakening is to amend the Constitution by adding a clause including the Lemon Test and the Everson Test as set rules. People should also begin to normalize the idea of religion and government being two completely separate things as philosophized by Roger Williams, for him, "Religious purity and good government were" "two separate and distinct concerns[578]" Only then will the U.S. Constitution be

---

[578]*Ibid.*, 299

protected in the way that religious liberty is protected in
the government.

THE MISCONCEPTION OF ORIGINALISM

BY JONATHAN SCHNEIDER

INTRODUCTION

Interpretations of the Constitution are often seen as dichotomous: originalism versus living constitutionalism.[579] Understandings of the interpretations themselves are also frequently reductive by viewing the former as adherent to a singular meaning and the latter as motivated entirely by subjective factors. This article will demonstrate how the line between these constitutional interpretations is far more convoluted.

WHAT CONSTITUTES AN ORIGINALIST INTERPRETATION?

Originalism refers to interpreting the Constitution by how it was originally written. However, perceptions of a document's original intent are inherently subjective,

---

[579] Originalism and living constitutionalism are referred to as points of view throughout this article. That is not to unwittingly propagate the dichotomy being critiqued, but to operate within the societal conception of each for the sake of practicality.

incumbent on the degree of interpretivism the text permits. A hypothetical amendment declaring that no chairs may be painted red, for example, would limit interpretations to a certain extent. Painting a chair crimson would undoubtedly be forbidden. However, whether the amendment meant to ban every shade within red's dominant wavelength, 625–740 nanometers on Georgia State University's "Spectral Colors" chart, or into the range of what is technically orange (610-624) would be up to interpretation.[580] Further complication could arise in the legality of using a paint that appears red through precise manipulation of hue, saturation, and brightness, the three factors which determine visible color.[581] Perhaps such manipulation would be disallowed by adherence, arguably, to what the amendment intended when it banned painting chairs red. Finally, one could debate whether the amendment meant that chairs cannot be completely painted red or that no red paint whatsoever may adorn them. Would a dime-sized spot of red qualify as painting the chair red? "Surely the Founders would have included 'with' or 'to any degree' if such absolutism was intended," hypothetical constitutional scholars could argue. Consequently, even within an amendment as relatively explicit as "chairs cannot be painted red," one's interpretation of the text dictates their stance on disputable areas.

[580] Nave, R. (n.d.). "Spectral Colors." Georgia State University From
https://web.archive.org/web/20171027012933/http://hyperphysics.phy-astr.gsu.edu/hbase/vision/specol.html.
[581] Nave, R. (n.d.). "Color Perception." Georgia State University From
http://hyperphysics.phy-astr.gsu.edu/hbase/vision/colper.html.

The hypothetical amendment evinces the crux of the issue in attempting to designate a singular interpretation of the Constitution "originalist," as the degree to which one is adherent to the text is constructed on their interpretation. Therefore, two self-professed originalists with divergent perceptions of a given amendment would likely reach contrasting conclusions on its intent. It is ultimately impossible to determine which is more originalist because, short of utilizing a time machine to ask the Founders a litany of clarifying questions, both viewpoints could be considered perfectly adherent to the text. Such a dynamic is particularly true when the text's meaning is highly disputed. For instance, take the Second Amendment:

"A well regulated Militia, being necessary to the security of a free State, the right of the people to keep and bear Arms, shall not be infringed."[582]

The comma separating the clauses (between "free State" and "the right") and the term "keep and bear Arms" allow profoundly contrasting perceptions of its meaning.[583] Discerning the second clause's relation to the first and what keeping and bearing arms in the first place entailed is perhaps the most effective way to reach a definitive answer for the genuinely originalist stance on the Second Amendment. That is an unenviable task since "keep and bear Arms" was a novel term when the Constitution was written, complicating the process of answering what the Founders meant with its use.[584]

---

[582] U.S. Const. amend. II.

[583] *Id.*

[584] Phillips, James C. & Blackman, Josh (2020). "The Mysterious Meaning of the Second Amendment." The Atlantic. From

ANALYZING AN "ORIGINALIST INTERPRETATION"

Examining originalism in the context of the Constitution's interpretive elements results in the conclusion that varied understandings are technically originalist. Justice Scalia describes a belief in one interpretation of the Second Amendment in the Court's *District of Columbia v. Heller* (2008) opinion, by his admission: "The prefatory clause [of the Second Amendment] comports with the Court's interpretation of the operative clause."[585] Interpretivism is demonstrable throughout the majority opinion, such as Justice Scalia utilizing *United States v. Miller*'s (1939) definition of the militia as "[comprising] all males physically capable of acting in concert for the common defense."[586] Furthermore, Justice Scalia uses the Court's opinion in *Miller* to establish the common use standard, determining which arms are protected by the Second Amendment.[587] Justice Scalia draws on precedent and "historical understanding" in each case.[588] However, the interpretive elements within the decision, such as the notion of *Miller*'s definition of the militia "[comporting]

---

https://www.theatlantic.com/ideas/archive/2020/02/big-data-second-amendment/607186/.

[585] *District of Columbia et al. v. Heller*, 554 U.S. 570 (2008).

[586] *District of Columbia et al. v. Heller*, 554 U.S. 570, 571 (2008).

[587] *District of Columbia et al. v. Heller*, 554 U.S. 570, 624 (2008). ("[O]rdinarily when called for [militia] service [able-bodied] men were expected to appear bearing arms supplied by themselves and of the kind in common use at the time.").

[588] *District of Columbia et al. v. Heller*, 554 U.S. 570, 625 (2008).

with founding-era sources," demonstrates the subjectivity within originalism.[589] Such subjectivity is equally reflected in what Justice Scalia decides not to include. For instance, the Second Militia Act of 1792 is cited as a specific "Founding-era [source]" with which *Miller*'s understanding of whom the militia entailed comports.[590] Notably, *Miller* drops the racial prerequisite for the militia detailed by the Act, which Justice Scalia quotes, as only extending membership to "free able-bodied white male [citizens] of the respective states."[591] Fortunately, Justice Scalia does not believe the Second Amendment applies exclusively to non-disabled white male citizens, despite such a position perhaps having the most significant "originalist" support from the Constitution and, in all likelihood, most "Founding-era sources."[592]

Justice Scalia defends the entirely subjective notion of common use similarly, writing: "[*Miller's* common use standard] finds support in the historical tradition of prohibiting the carrying of dangerous and unusual weapons."[593] What constitutes a "historical tradition" is not clarified. Nor is how such a standard should be employed as a mechanism within Constitutional law. The best faith interpretation is that Justice Scalia

---

[589] *District of Columbia et al. v. Heller*, 554 U.S. 570, 595 (2008).
[590] *Id.*
[591] George Washington's Mount Vernon (n.d.). "Militia Act of 1792." From

https://www.mountvernon.org/education/primary-sources-2/art icle/militia-act-of-1792/.
[592] *District of Columbia et al. v. Heller*, 554 U.S. 570, 595 (2008).
[593] *Id.*

believes the common use standard is supported by substantive due process, which allows courts to guard against government interference in cases concerning issues "so rooted in the traditions and conscience of our people as to be ranked as fundamental," which is, of course, subjective.[594] Therefore, Justice Scalia exhibits subjective interpretations of the Second Amendment in *District of Columbia v. Heller*, utilizing two concepts developed on an interpretive basis in *United States v. Miller*.

THE OSTENSIBLE DEMARCATION OF ADHERENCE TO PRECEDENT

One might argue that originalism views the Constitution's original intent alongside precedent, making its positions not mere interpretations but substantiated continuations of the Court's stance. Conversely, one might continue, even the Living Constitutionalists who base their position on an interpretation of the Constitution do not prioritize such a continuation, so despite technically being originalists by utilizing an interpretation of the Constitution's original intent, they are distinguishable from those who strictly adhere to precedent.

Notably, however, the originalist adherence to precedent is not absolute. For instance, Justice Scalia expressed that he would have ruled with the rest of the Court on *Brown v. Board of Education* (1954) if he was a Justice at the time.[595] That is despite it (rightfully) overruling

---

[594] *Snyder v. Massachusetts*, 291 U.S. 97, 105 (1934).
[595] Turner, Ronald (2014). "A Critique of Justice Antonin Scalia's Originalist Defense of *Brown v. Board of Education.*" UCLA Law Rev. From

Plessy v. Ferguson (1896) and arguably running counter to the 14th Amendment according to Justice Scalia's logic in justifying the Cconstitutional permissibility of the death penalty, for, as he says, it is "impossible to hold unconstitutional that which the Constitution explicitly contemplates."[596] Yet as Justice Breyer pointed out in a 2009 discussion between the two Justices at the University of Arizona: "It's certainly clear that at the time they passed the 14th Amendment... there was school segregation and they didn't think they were ending it."[597] One is inclined to wonder how *Brown v. Board* could rightfully deem segregation unconstitutional, in Justice Scalia's view, if it was explicitly contemplated and accepted by the 14th Amendment.[598]

Justice Scalia's response to cases like *Brown v. Board*, in which the Court included discernibly non-originalist "intangible considerations" in forming its decision, is that the overruled precedent was a misinterpretation of the Constitution: "A frequent line of attack against

---

https://www.uclalawreview.org/a-critique-of-justice-antonin-sc alias-originalist-defense-of-brown-v-board-of-education-2/.

[596] *Glossip v. Gross*, 576 U.S. 863, 894 (2015).

[597] James E. Rogers College of Law (2009). "U.S. Supreme Court Justices Antonin Scalia & Stephen Breyer Conversation on the Constitution." YouTube. From https://www.youtube.com/watch?v=jmv5Tz7w5pk&t=1385s. 19:57-20:09.

[598] To be clear, the critique is not that Justice Scalia agreed with the Court's decision in *Brown v. Board*. It is to note that even Justice Scalia, the foremost originalist in the Court's history, displayed inconsistencies in applying originalist principles, such as adherence to precedent and using that which is "explicitly contemplated" by the Constitution to determine constitutionality.

originalism consists in appeal to popular Supreme Court decisions that are assertedly based on a rejection of original meaning."[599] [600] Because *Plessy* betrays the original meaning of the 14th Amendment, he posits, overruling it merely constitutes a return to that meaning. Justice Scalia echoes a similar sentiment for other supposedly improperly decided cases, perhaps most famously concerning the ostensible creation of the right to privacy by *Griswold v. Connecticut* (1965) and the "judicially invented" right to abortion by *Roe v. Wade* (1973).[601]

In Justice Scalia's view, *Roe v. Wade* does not hold precedential value because it "declared unconstitutional state statutes that in no way contradicted any specific provision of the Constitution."[602] Consequently, Justice Scalia submits, *Roe* was wrongly decided and is a decision to be overruled instead of upheld.[603] However, Justice Scalia's argument that reversing allegedly non-precedential decisions, such as *Roe*, would be consistent with the Constitution's original meaning demonstrates the logically problematic nature of envisioning a single originalist interpretation: it does not exist. Thus, there is no logical limitation on viewing precedent as illegitimate within the given conception, as

---

[599] Scalia, Antonin & Garner, Bryan A. (2012). *Reading the Law: The Interpretation of Legal Texts*. West Group; 1st Edition. Pg. 162.
[600] *Brown v. Board of Education*, 347 U.S. 483, 493 (1954).
[601] *Lawrence v. Texas*, 539 U.S. 558, 586-87 (2003).
[602] Scalia & Garner, *supra* note 21, at 509.
[603] *Planned Parenthood of Southeastern Pa. v. Casey*, 505 U.S. 833, 980 (1992). ("The issue is whether [abortion] is a liberty protected by the Constitution of the United States. I am sure it is not.").

one's interpretation of the text is no less "originalist" than others, to an extent.

There are two distinct methods of constitutional interpretation, accepting the popular perception of originalism for argument's sake: originalism, which adheres to the original meaning of the text, and non-originalist interpretations, which stray from the text to varying degrees. Justice Scalia, operating within this dynamic, submits that reversing decisions reached by the latter is justified because they lack explicit constitutional support. For instance, the Court's decision in *Roe* was largely based on the right to privacy established by *Griswold v. Connecticut,* in which the Court writes: "[M]arital privacy... is within the penumbra of specific guarantees of the Bill of Rights," and *Eisenstadt v. Baird* (1972), which recognized the extension of the right to privacy to individuals.[604] [605] Therefore, Justice Scalia argues, originalism dictates that all three decisions do not have precedential value due to each utilizing solely implicit constitutional justification in determining and upholding the precise coverage of the "penumbra... of the Bill of Rights."[606] Consequently, overruling each decision supposedly results in more faithful adherence to the Constitution. Chief Justice Rehnquist's dissent in

---

[604] *Griswold v. Connecticut,* 381 U.S. 479, (1965).

[605] *Eisenstadt v. Baird,* 405 U.S. 438, 439 (1972). ("If under *Griswold, supra,* the distribution of contraceptives to married persons cannot be prohibited, a ban on distribution to unmarried persons would be equally impermissible, since the constitutionally protected right of privacy inheres in the individual, not the marital couple. If, on the other hand, *Griswold* is no bar to a prohibition on the distribution of contraceptives, a prohibition limited to unmarried persons would be under-inclusive and invidiously discriminatory.").

[606] *Griswold v. Connecticut,* 381 U.S. 479, (1965).

Planned Parenthood v. Casey (1992), with which Justices White, Scalia, and Thomas concurred, expresses such a position regarding *Roe*, beginning with: "We believe that *Roe* was wrongly decided, and that it can and should be overruled consistently with our traditional approach to stare decisis in constitutional cases."[607] Justice Scalia views *Griswold*, and *Eisenstadt* a fortiori due to its reliance on *Griswold*, similarly, saying the Court's decision was "wrong" in 2012.[608]

The evident issue with the position that adherence to precedent distinguishes the subjective views within originalism and living constitutionalism is that originalism only confers precedential value on decisions consistent with a given originalist interpretation. For instance, one could argue that a litany of decisions relating to the Second Amendment do not hold precedential value due to their interpretation, resulting in equally "originalist" positions for and against the restriction of firearms if each position is solely based on the text. The originalist can undoubtedly point to recent precedent to support their interpretation of the Second Amendment. However, by the same method that the originalist rejects *Roe v. Wade* and *Plessy v. Ferguson*, the living constitutionalist can merely argue that the Court improperly interpreted the Constitution in the decisions given as support. Such convolution is without including the additional complexity of cases that each "side" claims as support, such as *United States v. Miller*.

---

[607] *Planned Parenthood v. Casey*, 505 U.S. 833, 944 (1992).
[608] Hasen, Richard L (2018). *The Justice of Contradictions: Antonin Scalia and the Politics of Disruption*. Yale University Press. Pg. 96.

Thus, using adherence to chosen precedent as a demarcation is not only logically circular but entirely self-defeating, as the living constitutionalist can equally deem decisions inconsistent with their understanding of the text as forming illegitimate precedent. Such circularity blurs the ostensible distinction between originalists and living constitutionalists that follow an interpretation of the text, adherence to stare decisis, since that adherence is interpretive and incumbent on one's perception of the Constitution. Consequently, the only substantial separation between Justice Scalia's jurisprudence and that of "living constitutionalists" such as Justice Breyer is found in the particular constitutional interpretations on which they happen to disagree. To characterize the former as following or attempting to follow the Constitution's original meaning and the latter as not doing so, for better or worse, betrays a misunderstanding of the subjectivity within every constitutional interpretation. Finally, such a dichotomy is falsely predicated on the notion that the Constitution has an extant original meaning one can defend or assail.

THE ROLE OF DOCTRINES

Doctrinal adherence is another supposed approach by which one may distinguish originalists and living constitutionalists. Chief Justice Rehnquist, who championed a less constrained vision of originalism, alluded to Justice Souter's alleged straying from the doctrine of substantive due process in the Court's opinion for *Washington v. Glucksberg* (1997) due to Justice Souter advocating for the abandonment of the so-called traditional model of applying the doctrine. The two typical criteria, Chief Justice Rehnquist writes, are that the given right is "so rooted in the traditions and conscience of our people as to be ranked as fundamental" and a "'careful description' of the asserted fundamental liberty interest."[609] [610] Concurring with the Court's judgment that banning physician-assisted suicide does not violate the Due Process Clause, Justice Souter cites Justice Harlan's dissent in *Poe* v. *Ullman* (1961), examining whether the law was an "arbitrary [imposition]" or a "'purposeless [restraint]' at odds with the Due Process Clause."[611] However, Chief Justice Rehnquist writes, such an alternative approach "[W]ould largely abandon [the traditional] restrained methodology."[612] One might claim that Ooriginalism adheres to such "restrained doctrinal methodologies' ' whereas Living Constitutionalism abandons them.[613] Therefore, they may continue, originalists are more bound to precedent, despite deciding which decisions qualify as valid precedent, by the strict methodologies of doctrines. Justice Scalia demonstrates a similar belief in his *Lawrence v. Texas* (2003) dissent.[614] However, this position has two primary issues that weaken the

---

[609] *Washington v. Glucksberg*, 521 U.S. 702, 720-21 (1997), citing *Snyder* v. *Massachusetts*, 291 U.S. 97, 105 (1934) and *Reno v. Flores*, 507 U.S. 292, 302 (1993), respectively.

[610] *Reno v. Flores*, 507 U.S. 292, 302 (1993). ["'Substantive due process'" analysis must begin with a careful description of the asserted right, for '[t]he doctrine of judicial self-restraint requires us to exercise the utmost care whenever we are asked to break new ground in this field' (*Collins v. Harker Heights*, 503 U.S. 115, 125 (1992))."].

[611] *Washington v. Glucksberg*, 521 U.S. 702, 752 (1997), citing *Poe* v. *Ullman*, 367 U.S. 497, 543 (1961).

[612] *Washington v. Glucksberg*, 521 U.S. 702, 722 (1997).

[613] *Id.*

[614] *Lawrence v. Texas*, 539 U.S. 558, 586-87 (2003). ("I do not myself believe in rigid adherence to *stare decisis* in constitutional cases; but I do believe that we should be consistent rather than manipulative in invoking the doctrine.").

distinction between originalists and living constitutionalists.

The first problem with supposed adherence to doctrinal methodology bifurcating originalists and living constitutionalists is that alluding to doctrines, such as substantive due process, as having a thoroughly established historical methodology is often specious. For instance, Chief Justice Rehnquist's rebuke of Justice Souter's approach to substantive due process in *Washington v. Glucksberg* primarily uses six decisions to observe the existence of an "established method of substantive-due-process analysis."[615] *Snyder v. Massachusetts* (1934), *Palko v. Connecticut* (1937), and *Moore v. East Cleveland* (1977) are utilized to support the first criterion, while *Reno v. Flores* (1993), *Cruzan ex rel. Cruzan v. Director, Missouri Department of Health* (1990) and *Collins v. Harker Heights* (1992) support the second.[616] [617] It is curious, then, that Chief Justice Rehnquist recognizes the criteria as constituting a time-honored traditional approach by the Court, when the oldest decision supporting the latter criterion was seven years prior while the most recent of those supporting the former was nearly three times that. Undoubtedly, the precedential worth of a decision does not linearly depreciate based on its proximity to the present. However, the conjoining of criteria with supporting decisions made, on average, forty-seven and five years prior, respectively, to find an "established" doctrinal approach is notable.[618] More notable is Chief Justice Rehnquist, the "originalist" in this situation,

---

[615] *Washington v. Glucksberg*, 521 U.S. 702, 703 (1997).

[616] *Washington v. Glucksberg*, 521 U.S. 702, 722 (1997).

[617] *Id.*

[618] *Washington v. Glucksberg*, 521 U.S. 702, 703 (1997).

rebuking Justice Souter, the "living constitutionalist," for "[abandoning] the established [and] restrained methodology," the second criterion of which was based on decisions made less than a decade prior.[619] [620]

The second problem with utilizing adherence to doctrinal methodology to demarcate originalists and living constitutionalists is that such a function ignores the subjective nature with which precedential value is granted. For instance, Justice Scalia frequently lambasted the "judicially invented" right to abortion and the right to privacy found by the Court in *Roe v. Wade* and *Griswold v. Connecticut*, respectively.[621] [622] Justice Scalia explains that "*Griswold* expressly disclaimed any reliance on the doctrine of 'substantive due process,' and grounded the so-called 'right to privacy' in penumbras of constitutional provisions other than the Due Process Clause," while *Roe* regarded abortion as a "'fundamental right' protected by the Due Process Clause."[623] Yet *Griswold* also notes that the case matter "lies within the zone of privacy created by several fundamental constitutional guarantees," weakening the notion that the Court's decision was singularly rooted in the perceived "penumbra… of the Bill of Rights."[624] *Griswold* also cites several cases that potentially demonstrate the right to privacy's status as a "principle of justice so rooted in the traditions and conscience of our people as to be ranked as fundamental," arguably meriting substantive due process protection, such as *Boyd* v. *United States*

---

[619] *Washington v. Glucksberg*, 521 U.S. 702, 722 (1997).
[620] *Washington v. Glucksberg*, 521 U.S. 702, 703 (1997).
[621] *Lawrence v. Texas*, 539 U.S. 558, 586-87 (2003).
[622] *Lawrence v. Texas*, 539 U.S. 558, 595 (2003).
[623] *Id.*
[624] *Griswold v. Connecticut,* 381 U.S. 479, 485 (1965).

(1886), *NAACP* v. *Alabama* (1958), and *Mapp* v. *Ohio* (1961).[625] [626] However, Justice Scalia largely ignores the historical support for the right to privacy, which, as Justices O'Connor, Kennedy, and Souter note in the Court's opinion for *Planned Parenthood v. Casey*, has a history extending at least to *Union Pacific R. Co. v. Botsford* (1891).[627] Therefore, adherence to doctrinal methodology, much like the precedent formed by individual decisions, is built on the perceived precedential value of the relevant cases. Consequently, one's adherence to the so-called traditional approach of a given doctrine is similarly incumbent on the constitutional interpretation to which they subscribe, and thus equally worthless in providing an "objective" demarcation.

CONCLUSION

As with the hypothetical amendment banning chairs from being painted red, specific interpretations of the Constitution are decidedly non-originalist. For instance, arguing that the creators of such an amendment meant "paint red" as a figure of speech alluding to the text's

---

[625] *Snyder v. Massachusetts*, 291 U.S. 97, 105 (1934).

[626] The Court also cites *Skinner* v. *Oklahoma* (1942), *Breard* v. *Alexandria* (1951), *Public Utilities Comm'n* v. *Pollak* (1952), *Frank* v. *Maryland* (1959), *Monroe* v. *Pape* (1961), and *Lanza* v. *New York* (1962) as support for the right to marital privacy found in *Griswold* (*Griswold v. Connecticut*, 381 U.S. 479, 485 (1965)).

[627] *Planned Parenthood of Southeastern Pa. v. Casey*, 505 U.S. 833, 926 (1992), citing *Union Pacific R. Co. v. Botsford*, 141 U.S. 250, 251 (1891). "([N]o right is held more sacred, or is more carefully guarded by the common law, than the right of every individual to the possession and control of his own person, free from all restraint or interference of others. . . .").

actual meaning, such as forbidding the murder of someone sitting in a chair, is in demonstrable contravention with the intent of the amendment. That is to say that this article is not arguing that any interpretation of the Constitution is equally originalist. Instead, it is to recognize that there is a measure of subjectivity in every interpretation of the Constitution, especially if the text's original meaning is nebulous. Furthermore, the use of precedent to supposedly separate originalists from living constitutionalists ignores the inherently subjective nature of originalism determining whether a given decision has precedential value, in both individual decisions and doctrines. Thus, using precedent to support an interpretation, but only valuing precedent when it affirms one's position, argues that one's interpretation is correct because of one's interpretation, since any contradictory decision does not hold precedential value. Therefore, attributing "originalist" status to a given interpretation and declaring every other view "living constitutionalist" is wholly unfounded.

Made in the USA
Middletown, DE
25 July 2022